Autobiography

of an

Elderly Woman

"As soon as you feel too old to do a thing,
do it,"—Margaret Deland.

Autobiography

of an

Elderly Woman

Anonymous

Afterword by

Doris Grumbach

For information address
Pushcart Press
P.O. Box 380
Wainscott, NY 11975

ISBN: 0-916366-79-0

Distributed by W. W. Norton & Co., 500 Fifth
Avenue, New York, New York 10110

Printed in the United States of America

Contents

Autobiography

of an

Elderly Woman

The Shadow
of Age

As I look back over my life, it divides itself into four parts. First come all the years before I married, and as I look back on my childhood and my short girlhood, it seems to me as though I were remembering the life of some other woman, for during these many years I know that I have changed several times from one person to another, and the world about me has had time to change also. All that early part swims in a fog, with here and there events popping out of the mist, more distinct than those a week past — often meaningless and trivial these; I cannot tell by what caprice memory has elected to keep them so clear. Lately I find myself returning to certain opinions and prejudices of my girlhood, that I had long forgotten. Time, after all, has not obliterated them, nor have I walked away from them. It is rather as though I had gone in a circle, and as I come to the completion of it I find my old thoughts and opinions, changed and grown older, waiting for me.

With my marriage begins the part of my life that seems real to me — it is as if I had dreamed all that went before. I loved the time when my children were little, and I have often wished that I could put them and myself back in the nursery again. I pity the women whose children come too late for them all to be in some sense children together. But however young a mother is, there is a great gap between her and her babies. My little children were of a different generation from me. And for all our striving to understand, they were babies and my husband and I "grown people," though as I look back we seem mere boy and girl.

We worried over our babies — there were four of them, all in the nursery at the same time — we sat up nights gravely discussing their "tendencies," and their education — only to find that the very tendencies over which we worried most they outgrew, and that when the time for education began in earnest, all the conditions had changed and new methods had been evolved.

It will always be this way — mothers and fathers will always sit up late nights, as we did, discussing the "futures" of their little two-year-old sons.

We tried so hard to do right; we thought back through the years and said:

"I felt this and this when I was little. I thought this way and this — such and such things frightened me. My father seemed unjust when he punished me for this offense; my mother made such and such mistakes. I will not make these mistakes with my children."

And so, thinking to avoid all the mistakes of our own parents, we made, all unknowing, fresh mistakes of our own.

When I was little, for instance, I was very much afraid of the dark; so much so that the fears of my childhood haunted my whole life — an unlighted staircase has terrors for me even to this day. And I made up my mind that no child of mine should suffer from fear of darkness as I did. So my first child had a light in his room. He was always naughty about going to bed, and he grew to be a big boy before I found out that this was because the gray twilight of the room was horrible to him, and that he was very much afraid of the uncertain shapes of the furniture he saw in the dim light of the lamp, though not at all afraid of the dark. It is with such well-intentioned blunders that one brings up one's children.

Grandmothers know that this is so, and for that reason all the various "systems" seem like foolish words to them. They have learned that there will be mistakes made where there are parents and children — yes, and that there will be cruelties and injustices, and that the only way to deal with very little children is to love them very much and let them feel this love.

The time my children took in growing up seems to me phenomenally short; one day they were babies and the next they were young people to be reckoned with, having wills and personalities of their own. Other mothers tell me that their children grew up as quickly, but this I have hard work to believe.

When my oldest son was nearly a man and the others crowding on his heels, my dear husband died, and my son grew up overnight, and in the next few years — years that were very full ones, for all their sadness — my other children stole a march on me and grew up too; almost, I might say, behind my back. While I was taking on myself the new responsibilities of my so altered life, and while the world seemed yet very empty of companionship, I found that my children were becoming my comrades, and so I entered on the third quarter of my life.

My boys and girls all at once belonged to my generation; we had common interests, common tastes and amusements — for all practical purposes we were the same age. It was at this time that the warning voice sounded in my ear, but I seemed to myself almost as young as my children, so no wonder I didn't recognize it as the voice of age calling to me. It is a very pleasant time when one is still on the great stage of life, playing one's small part shoulder to shoulder with one's children; shoulder to shoulder, too, with people a score of years one's senior. This is the golden moment when time holds its breath for a while and one imagines that, however old one may get, one will forever stay in spirit at the same smiling "middle way." Age, considered at that time, seems rather the result of some accident or some weakness of will than the result of living a great number of years in the world. So for many years my children and I did our work side by side, I helping and advising them, they aiding and advising me in the common partnership of our lives.

The fourth part of my life, my present life about which I am going to write, began when again I became of a different generation from my children — with the difference that they now are the strong, I the weak; that they treasure me and care for me, worry over me and weep over me — a spry old lady, and, I am afraid, sometimes a defiant old lady, impatient of the rules which they lay down for me, as once they were of the rules that I made for them.

Elderly Woman

How did this come about? When did it happen?

There was a time when I was more of a comrade than a mother to my daughters; when I was the adviser of my sons. Now I am not. I do not know when the change came, nor do they, if indeed they realize it at all. There was a time when I was of their generation, now I am not. I cannot put my finger on the time when old age finally claimed me. But there came a moment when my boys were more thoughtful of me, when they didn't come to me any more with their perplexities, not because I had what is called "failed," but because they felt that the time had come when I ought to be "spared" every possible worry. So there is a conspiracy of silence against me in my household. "We mustn't worry mother," is the watchword of my dear children, and the result of their great care is that I am on the outside of their lives.

Shadows come and go among them; they talk about them; I feel the chill of their trouble, but I'm never told what it's about. Before me they keep cheerful; when I come, the shadow passes from their faces and they talk with me about all the things that they think will interest me. I move in a little artificial, smiling world away from all the big interests of life. If one of them is sick away from home, I am not told until it is all over; if there is any crisis among them, they do all they can to keep me from hearing of it. But in the end I always do know, for no one can live in the shadow of any anxiety and not be aware of it.

So the great silence enfolds me more and more. I live more alone and solitary among those I love, groping in the silence, watching the faces of my children to find what is passing in their lives. I often think how sweet it would have been if my husband had lived, and we could have grown old together, understanding and giving companionship to each other.

I can remember the very day when I *realized* that age had claimed me at last. There is a great difference between being a thing and realizing it. A woman may say a hundred times that she is ugly; she may be ugly; but unless she realizes that she is ugly; it will make very little difference. It is the consciousness of our defects which undoes us — and so with age.

Elderly Woman

This great readjustment began with the most trivial of events. I happened to see a little dust on the table and around on the bric-a-brac — it seems to me that dusting is a lost art — and I was just wiping it off. I was enjoying myself, for I belong to a generation which was taught to work with its hands and to delight in doing its work nicely, when I heard Margaret's step on the stairs; she is my youngest daughter, home on a visit. My first impulse was to sit down and pretend to be reading, but I resolved to brazen it out — after all, there is no reason why I shouldn't dust my own bric-a-brac in my own home if I choose.

She came into the parlor.

"*What* are you doing, darling?" she said.

"I am dusting the vases on the mantel," I answered, and I tried to keep any note of guilt from my voice.

"Why couldn't you have called Annie?" she asked me, with tender reproach.

"I like to stir around myself sometimes," I said, and for the life of me I couldn't help being a little defiant.

"Well, then, why couldn't you let me do it?

You might have called me," she went on in the same tone.

"I told you I like to do it."

"It isn't good for you to stand on your feet so much. Give me that duster, mother. You'll tire yourself all out."

"I get tired *sitting*," I broke out.

"I always have said that you ought to take more exercise in the open air." By this time she had taken away my duster. "Why don't you go out and take a little walk? Come — I'll go with you."

Presently she had finished dusting, but I saw ever so many little places that I should have to wipe up later on, furtively. I should have enjoyed finishing that dusting myself.

"I'll run up and get your things," said Margaret.

Now, I cannot abide having any one trifle with my bureau drawers, and it isn't because I'm old enough to have middle-aged sons and daughters, either. Ever since I can remember, I have put my things away myself. I keep my bonnets in the little drawers and my gloves and veils — my everyday ones, that is — beside them; and I know that I shall never be able to find anything again once Margaret has been among them. Besides that, I do not like going to walk. Walking aimlessly for exercise has always seemed most futile to me; a feeble stroll that has no objective point, not even the post office, annoys me more than any other way of spending my time. I have never walked except when I had something to walk for, and I don't intend to begin at my time of life.

"I don't think I'll go to walk, dear. I'm going out this afternoon —"

Now, though I said this indifferently enough, in a tone which didn't invite discussion, yet I braced myself inwardly; I knew what was coming.

"Oh, mother darling," my daughter cried. "You're not going to that lecture, with your cold, in that drafty hall! And you always catch more cold in a crowd! You won't go, will you?"

"Well, well —" I temporized.

"You won't go — promise."

Then the door-bell rang, and I made my escape to my own room and locked my door after me. I knew well enough what would happen — how Margaret would tell the others at dinner that I was going out, and how they would protest. And I made up my mind, as I often have before, that since I am old enough to know what is best for me, I would go to that lecture, let them talk as they might; so I got ready for the battle, resolving for the hundredth time that I would not be run by my children.

As I sat in my room plotting — yes, plotting — how I should outwit my daughter, it came over me what a funny thing it was that I should be contriving to get my own way, for all the world like a naughty, elderly child, while my daughter was worrying about my headstrong ways as if she were my mother instead of my being hers.

How increasingly often I hear as the years go on, not only from my own children, but from other people whose mothers are already old: "Mother will not take care of herself!" And then follow fearsome stores of mother's latest escapade — just as one tells how naughty Johnnie is getting and how Susie kicks her bedclothes off — stories of how mother made a raid on the attic and cleaned it almost single-handed when all the family were away; stories of clandestine descents into the perilous depths of the cellar; hair-raising tales of how mother was found on a stepladder hanging a window curtain; how mother insisted on putting down the preserves and pickles — rows and rows and rows of shining glasses of them — herself, and how tired she was afterwards, as if putting down the preserves tired only women who were past middle age. And a certain indignation rose within me as I remembered that I can visit my own attic and my own cellar only by stealth or with a devoted and tyrannical child of mine standing over me to see that I don't "overdo." For the motto of all devoted sons and daughters is: "Nag mother to death, if necessary, but don't let her overdo."

Well, what if I should overdo? Before one is old, one is allowed to shorten one's life unchecked; one may have orgies of work undisturbed. And I, for one, would far rather shorten my life by overdoing than have it lengthened out by a series of mournful, inactive years. Again I said I would not be run by my children,

And as I got to this point in my meditation I heard my son Dudley coming up the stairs. I knew he would come to see me, so I unlocked my door.

I had said that I would not be run by my children. Now see to what depths constant nagging reduces a naturally straightforward woman. I know that Dudley watches me very closely, and I often wish he would sometimes ignore my moods as I do his; but this time I was ready for him, pulling a long face when he came in.

He said at once — I knew he would —

"You look blue, old girl."

"I never," I burst out, "can do the least thing without you children interfering. I can't read *all* the time, you know; but whenever I proposed to do anything, I meet with such opposition that for the sake of peace I give up at once."

I spoke more warmly than I felt as far as this particular instance was concerned, for I was fighting for a principle.

"Who's been bothering you?" Dudley demanded.

Elderly Woman

"It isn't 'bothered' I've been," I remonstrated. "It's that you children are needlessly anxious about me. It's far better for me to go out now and then than to sit in the house from morning till night. And what's more," I added determinedly, "I am going to the lecture this afternoon no matter what Margaret or any one else says!"

Dudley laughed.

"There, there," he said, patting my hand. "You *shall* go; no one is going to oppose you. You'll go if I have to take you there in a carriage myself."

So I knew I had won the day, for in our family Dudley is the important member. But I made up my mind, just the same, that I would go on my own two feet to that lecture, for there was no need at all of a carriage. And I did go, alone and walking, though I slipped out of the front door so quietly that it was hardly dignified —"sneaked," was what Margaret called it.

As Dudley went down the hall, I thought how a similar warfare is being carried on all over this country to-day, wherever there are elderly mothers and middle-aged sons and daughters — the children trying to dominate their parents with the end in view of making them take abnormal care of their health, and the older people fighting ever more feebly and petulantly for their lost independence. Not only struggling to have their own way, not only chafing at the leading-strings in which their watchful, devoted children would keep them, but fighting, too, for the little glimmer of youth that is yet left them.

For all this care by one's children means but one thing, and that is — age. While you slept, old age came upon you. You count the number of your years by the way your daughter watches your steps, and you see your infirmities in your son's anxious eyes; and the reason of all this struggle — why our own attics and cellars are forbidden ground to us; why our daughters take our dusters from us and tenderly nag us — is that they are valiantly, if tactlessly, striving to delay by their care the hour which they know must come, while we try to ignore its approach.

We like to kill the days, which sometimes crawl past us so slowly, with an illusion of activity, and we do not like to be reminded day by day, hour by hour, that we are old, that there is no work we need do, no "ought" calling us any more; that our work in the world is being done by other people and our long vacation has already begun.

As I sat alone that evening and soberly went over the events of the day, I clearly realized the meaning of Margaret's taking away my duster. I realized that there was no work in the world that I ought to do but take care of myself. I realized that I was old; and from that day, though I often forget it, the world has looked a little different to me; my point of view has, in some subtle way, shifted. It was on that day that I sat down to think how it was that I had come to be old and what the invisible milestones were that I had passed along the way.

The first time age touched me it was with so light a finger that I did not recognize the touch; I didn't know what had happened. Indeed, the touch of age at first irritated me; then I laughed at it, and finally I became a little bewildered, realizing confusedly that a new element had come into my life to stay. But I did not know that it was the shadow of age which was upon me, that it was always there, invisible, quiet, persistent, and, patient as death, waiting to claim me.

This first touch of age comes when our children begin to dictate to us.

The other day I saw the youth of a woman begin to wither under my very eyes. She didn't know what was happening, but I knew what shadow was over her. To me she seems young, for I have seen her grow up, and though she has big daughters, I never thought of her as approaching middle age until the last time she and the girls came to see me.

Edith is a big, handsome, buoyant woman, but there was a subdued air about her for which I couldn't account until her eldest daughter said sweetly, but with decision:

"Mother isn't looking well; she ought to have some sea air."

And Edith replied with the note of helpless irritation that I have come to know so well:

"I have told the children so often that I dislike leaving my comfortable home in the summer."

Elderly Woman

Then I knew why Edith seemed changed: her children had begun to run her.

So the finger of age touches all of us in much the same fashion. The warning may not always come through some dear child, though with mothers it is oftenest in that way; but the voice of the valiant new generation speaks in one way or another to every man and woman, and from the moment you have heard that voice you have set your face old-agewards, though twenty years or more may pass before you are really old. The strong new generation, eager and clamorous, is at your heels ready to take your place, anxious to perform your tasks. Already your children are altering the world that you know; already they are meditating the changes that they will make when the reins of power fall into their hands; and one day you will wake up in a new world, an unhomelike place to which you must adjust yourself as a baby must adjust himself to his surroundings, but with the difference that every day the baby makes progress, whereas every day you will find the new conditions harder to understand — as I have, and as your mother has.

After my husband's death I was very anxious to have my own mother make her home with me, and at the time I couldn't understand why she wouldn't. Now I know. She lived instead in a little house in the town where she had spent her life, and for all companionship she had a "girl" nearly as old as herself. We used to worry about her a great deal, about her loneliness, her lack of care of herself — all the things that my children worry about now; but she met all our pleading to live with us with the baffling smile, and the "Well, well, we'll see," that she had used with us when we were little children.

One time I accompanied her home after a visit she had made us, in spite of her protests that it was ridiculous for me to do so. It had stormed and the roads were bad, and I was afraid to let her travel alone. She strode ahead of me, straight as a pine tree, up the brick path which led to her house, and opened the front door. The gesture of welcome she gave her lonely little home, and the long breath she drew, as of relief, I didn't then understand, though I always remembered them. I understand now. She had come back to herself, to her own life, to her memories. Here she could think her own thoughts and lead her life as she wished. She could even sit in a draft without an affectionately officious child following her up with a shawl, and her little home, lonely as it was, was less lonely than the strange world we lived in. I have often taken the duster from my mother's hands as Margaret did from mine the other morning. And I suppose the same little drama will be enacted in every family until the end of time by mothers and daughters.

My Mother's House

As my years crowd upon me, I read the meaning of certain things in the past that as a young woman I never understood, for there is nothing more variable than our past. Young people regard the happenings of yesterday as a fixed quantity, but the past is just as insecure as the future, for all events have meaning and gather value only according to the personality they visit. This being so, as time changes, the tragedy of yesterday softens and smiles at one. The small and meaningless event, in the light of those which follow it, grows and grows until it overshadows all.

Elderly Woman

The boundaries that fix life itself — birth and death — are perhaps the only events that keep their primary importance with us as we age. Mysterious is the past and strange and fortuitous. It veils its face like the future. We cannot remember what we will; we forget the very things that we have loved and felt and suffered. The memory of the emotions passes from us, and it is as if they had never been. Why should I keep this trivial memory and discard the other? Who can tell me? I know that this and that, when I was a girl, made my heart beat; this I remember, but not with my emotions. Why it beat is now mysterious to me.

As I grow old I find myself in a thousand looks and gestures of my mother, the memories of which come crowding to me out of the past. We go down to the grave as egotists; so it is the mother of her later years who now returns to me as I tread over the path she trod.

Especially significant is her house — the little place so liberally fenced in and not thrown into the next place in the modern and odious fashion. Up the side of the brick path were posy beds — for that is the true name for such a garden, — and posy beds there were in front of the house, and behind grew other flowers. These my mother tended herself; the lawn was cared for by a gardener. This man was a great thorn in the side of all of us who visited her. He spent his days gossiping cheerily over the fence, telling the neighbors details like the difference between the thermometer in the shade and in the sun. He would communicate to them at what hour he had arisen that morning and how his hens were laying. His cheerful and ceaseless babble went on whenever he found an ear to receive it. This old man annoyed us, as I said. He was a kindly soul, and we had no objection to him as an individual, but his prattle bored us, and we felt that he should work for the stipend he received for mowing the lawn and raking up the leaves. This feeling our mother did not share; she was contented to let him dawdle through the hours of the day if he chose, so that some time or other the lawn was cut; and as she pottered about her flowers, gloves on her hands and a wide shade hat on her head — for she was of the generation whose gentlewomen were taught to be careful of their complexion and their hands, and thought it unbecoming in a delicate female to get blowzy with sunburn and blackened with tan — she would stop and talk with him.

We would point out to her that she was encouraging him in his idle habits, and were always ready at a moment's notice to furnish her with a strong likely boy of eighteen in place of this doddering and garrulous individual. I can remember conversations like this:

"Mother, I've heard that Widow Johnson's boy wants to work —"

"Widow Johnson's boy! That weedy beanpole — all legs!"

"He's eighteen —"

"I know your eighteen-year-olds," my mother would cry. "They stop working the moment your back is turned. I like my man; I can depend on him."

"Yes," we would reply bitterly, "you can depend on him to do nothing. Besides, you'll be helping the boy's mother."

We knew that a practice of my mother's was to help along solitary women less fortunately placed than she had been.

But to this suggestion she would reply with a masterful definiteness:

"I'm not an eleemosynary institution, my dear."

There was no arguing with her; there was no making her see that that was precisely what she was. There was no use offering her men in the prime of life to mow her lawn any more than there was in offering her what she called "tittering and hooting boys."

She was just as bad about the bits of carpentry that there were to be done around the house. There was a certain workman who came occasionally on odd jobs and whom we tried to have her get rid of, but for whom, after all, we had a sneaking fondness.

I can remember this old man well. He seemed no thicker than a piece of paper and gave the impression of some odd ghost, so bent-over was he, so pale — a strange, tanned pallor, framed in by tenuous hair and sparse, white whiskers. He moved brokenly and feebly, and yet clung with the tenacity of a fly to the side of a roof. He liked shingling, he said; it kept him young. This I doubt, nor have I ever yet tried it for the disease of age.

My mother claimed he was a good carpenter. That may have been; at any rate, all the carpentering that was done, was done by him, from shingling to pottering over a broken piazza rail. What especially irritated us about him was that his memory had departed from him. It was impossible for him to remember for ten consecutive minutes where to find his tools. One could find him at any unexpected place, always, he said, looking for the nails or the screwdriver or the hammer. He strewed them about him with as lavish a gesture as Millet's Sower, so one might judge from the length of time he spent looking for them. He would wander from room to room, peering with near-sighted eyes into every corner; and sometimes he would forget which tool it was he had lost, and would have to go back to find out, and then begin the search all over again. He never became impatient at this, but continued his long wanderings like some little New England "Wandering Jew," in sorrow over the unnatural perversity of his tools rather than in any anger against them.

A third person my mother employed of this same kind; this one a painter. He was elderly also; garrulous, but in a different way from the childlike prattle of the gardener.

No, he couldn't tell how much a thing would cost. Perhaps it would cost so much, and perhaps so much; he couldn't tell until he got through. No, he couldn't tell you how long it would take him — perhaps a day, perhaps longer — he didn't know. When would he come? He didn't know; maybe tomorrow — maybe next day — he couldn't tell.

"But," my mother would persist, "we've got to have that kitchen floor painted and we've got to know when you're coming, Mr. Bunner."

"Well, now, Mis' Paine, I can't tell you. Now, I'll tell you how it is; I'm waitin' now for some paint to paint Malcolm's house, an' when I get that paint, I'll paint his house, an' when I get that done, I'll do your kitchen."

"But while you're waiting," my mother would urge.

And you can imagine us fairly tramping up

and down with rage, wishing to poke forth from the doors the old piker.

And thus it would go on, and after spending more or less of kindliness on him, my mother would at last persuade the old man to come the next day.

As I look back on it, it seems as if always one or the other of these feckless elderly workmen was engaged in doing some odd job or other around my mother's place, and I think this was very likely true. I know now why she did it; it gave her that feeling with which we older people like to deceive ourselves, — and succeed according to the clearness of our mental capacity — the illusion of activity, of really accomplishing something; and my mother accomplished this: that she kept up her house spick and span to her last moment. I know now, too, why she had these elderly people about her, and why she couldn't abide the smart, modern methods of younger and more efficient people. Not only had they worked for her for years and she had a loyalty towards her own generation, but I think she had some deeper sympathy and liking for their failing powers.

Possibly she saw her own mirrored in theirs; perhaps she remembered when the old carpenter was as spry as a kitten and when he never so much as mislaid a hook-eye.

They were old and she was old, but they were older than she, and I think that the contrast between them gave her a sense of youthful power. I have seen an aged mother be almost a fountain of youth. There lives here an old woman who is upwards of ninety, and with her live her unmarried daughters — women well along in their sixties. The old lady still calls her daughters "the girls," and orders them about smartly. They are all of the old school and they obey her very well, but in turn they tyrannize over her, look after her, "do for her," as we have it here. One can never drop in on them without their having a story to tell about some new rash deed of "mother's"; and so they are young in spirit, having a work to do in the world; some one to run, and no chit of a younger generation to run them. Another reason for their youthfulness is that the house has not had so much as a new matchsafe for twenty years: they yet have about them things all of their own choosing; they have not had to part with the familiar friends of their youth.

My mother's house was like this While she was particular about repairs, new things she would not buy. Within-doors, combined with an austere order, there was a certain dilapidation of armchairs due to over-use; the lamp was old; everything about her had been used for years, and the presents which we made her stuck out like so many sore thumbs — I am sure that many of them disappeared into cupboards and drawers when we took our departure.

And when we broke up our larger house in which we lived, and she and father came to live in this little one, I remember she gave us with lavish hand what seemed to us the pick of the furniture, and kept for herself those things that belonged to her earlier years.

Have you ever noticed when it is that people have their houses "done over"? I have. It usually occurs soon after the daughters have been "out" a while, and have had time to develop a taste of their own. Then the moment comes when the furniture is rearranged, new touches are added, old-fashioned things sent away to the attic for a long rest, and the house passes from the older generation to the younger. The altered aspect of the house shows that the young people are beginning to take possession of their own. Do you remember when so many of the parlor carpets throughout the land were done away with and little slippery rugs put in their places? And a wonder it is that we didn't all break our necks sliding across the floor on them!

I have an old friend who picks her way gingerly across the shining, polished floor, as much in fear for her poor stiff bones as if she were walking on ice. As she walks carefully from one treacherous oasis of a rug to another and deposits herself on a Chippendale chair, I can but remember the time when the room was full of billowy, upholstered chairs, faulty in line, perhaps, but holding out ample, inviting arms to you. And as she perches herself on the uncompromising colonial furniture, I know that she regrets her comfortable old chairs, though she bravely pretends she thinks the new furniture a great improvement.

Elderly Woman

Here is another of the milestones of age; we pretend as hard as we can that we like many things we don't like, that we may not seem old-fashioned to our dear ones. We do what we can to keep pace with them until our old legs are weary with running; but our children, do the best we may, are far in advance of us. We make concession after concession of our own preferences, even to giving up the things that lived with us when we were young and which grew old with us and old-fashioned even as we did. To please our children we treacherously discard them, pretending we think them, in their old-fashioned comfort, as hideous as do our young people. My friend points out the purity of design of the new furniture, but she has had one of the old parlor chairs done over and put in her own bedroom. She sits there a good deal. I have noticed that older women work and read much in their own rooms, and I sometimes wonder if it isn't because the rest of the house has become strange and unhomelike.

The Conventions
of Age

I can remember when I was a young woman how many of my mother's foibles fretted me, for I was like the rest. I hadn't reasoned it out any more than most people do, but I held some immutable opinions about the conduct of age. If I had my life to live over again, I should know better. I should cherish each of my mother's restless days, because I would know that her very restlessness and occasional discontent were the signs that life was keen within her, and that I myself had made her restless, because as a too zealous daughter I had in a measure, together with Time, taken from her some of the occupations that still by right belonged to her. I would let her have her way on all the minor points of dress and occupation. I would not criticize the old workmen she chose; and, above all, I would not try to impose on her any of my ideas of how an older woman should act. For young people have hard-and-fast notions concerning older women's actions. When we depart from them, they make a personal grievance of it.

I do not think I am exaggerating when I say that there is no class of society so bound down by convention, and for no good reason, as are the oldest of all. A young and pretty woman must, of course, walk carefully along life's paths; she must take care to avoid even the appearance of evil. As she grows older, a suitable amount of convention in the mother of a family is a wholesome balance. But when a woman grows old, when she has climbed the ladder of years beyond the point where scandal could touch her, one would think that she might lay aside minor conventions of life; that at last she might do what she pleased, only limited by her own failing strength. There are so few things, after all, left for us to do, so few that we have the heart left for, or the wish for now, that it would seem only right that we should follow our caprice in the small matters that still belong to us.

I recently heard a young woman my daughter's age complain somewhat after this fashion:

"There are no more real grandmothers left in the world! I don't know what the nowadays children are going to do. How much my dear old grandmother meant to me! As far back as I can remember, her sweet white head, crowned with its snow-white cap, was always at her favorite window in summer, and in winter she sat beside the open fire with her feet upon a little hassock, like Whistler's mother. We children always knew where to find grandma. She was always so glad when we came. I can see yet the welcome in her eyes when we would run in on her. She would invent little games for us and tell us little stories as long as we would stay. The lovely part of it was that she was always *there*. No matter if mother was out, or any one else, we could be sure of finding *grandma* ready to hear all about our little joys and troubles."

During this little recital, which, of course, was not a long peroration, but was given to us in the broken phrases of a conversation, I had a very vivid picture of this old lady, probably only a few years older than myself, who was "always there." What infirmity, I wondered, made her be there all the time? When an older woman is "always there," depend upon it, there is some deeper reason and a sadder one than that she was waiting for her little grandchildren. No one knows this better than I myself, for I, too, am "there," for one reason or another, more than I wish to be. Oh, I knew very well how eagerly she waited for those little grandchildren of hers, and how the lonely, gray, spacious hours brightened up in the flicker of their laughter. I knew, too, as they got over being little babies, how brief their sweet, tumultuous visits must have been. It is only very little children who spend much time in their grandmother's skirts. For a long time past I have been conscious that Betty only stays with me when she is kept in or has nothing better to do. Once a child has grown into liberty, you may be sure it will not spend overlong spaces of time with its grandparents, unless they, too, are active enough to be in the field, like an old English friend of mine who, at seventy-three, with undimmed enthusiasm, is teaching his grandchildren to ride and shoot and whip a trout stream. You may depend upon it that they idolize him, not because he is "there" all the time, but because he can do all these things better than they can, and is, besides, a living spring of fishing-tackle, rods, and other sporting goods.

But this was not all my friend had to say. After her picture of her own poor grandmother, she took up the first part of the argument.

"Nowadays," said she, "I look around in vain for sweet old ladies like my grandmother. There do not seem to *be* any old ladies any more; they seem to have gone out of fashion along with the dear, pretty caps they used to wear, and that they looked so sweet in. Nowadays older women dress just like their daughters. Instead of ever being where their grandchildren can find them, they are off, if you please, at clubs or playing cards or even taking a jaunt in a motor-car!"

She said this, mind you, under my very nose, and I didn't know whether I was vaguely pleased with the subtle flattery that she ignored the fact that I was a very case in point of her recalcitrant new-fangled grandmother, or whether to feel a little vexed with her for being so obtuse. For a moment I entertained the idea of allowing myself the luxury of playing at being her age, and then I felt I had better come out flat-footed, and say, "Well, Eleanor, I suppose you think I had better wear a cap and give up the whist club"; but I knew she would answer, with a look of naïve wonder in her soft brown eyes, "Why, auntie, *you're* not old!" So all I said was, "I suppose, my dear, the conditions of life are easier and the doctors are better, so nowadays many older people manage to keep their infirmities at bay a little longer."

I think that back of Eleanor's ideal of a grandmother there lay a good deal of unconscious selfishness. An elderly mother who sits contentedly by the fire all day is a far smaller responsibility than a mother that one can never put a hand on, and who, at a moment's notice, goes off on perilous expeditions.

Everything Eleanor had said about her grandmother had ruffled me more than it should, so after I got over my impatience, I asked myself why I had been so annoyed, after all. I found the answer soon enough. In lamenting that there were no grandmothers left like hers, Eleanor had clearly defined the position that the average person takes toward older women.

Each generation permits a different type of young girl, but the older woman must not change; her outline is fixed and immovable. She must be like Eleanor's grandmother, "always there"— waiting, waiting, with a smiling face through the long, quiet, empty hours, for her grandchildren to come home.

I read a clever poem the other day, the refrain of which was, "I'm looking forward to old age."

"Then," said the young writer, "at last I can

be perfectly comfortable. I can lay aside the minor conventions along with my tight shoes and tight corsets. I can at last do as I please. I'm looking forward to old age."

When this young woman arrives at the Land of Old Age, though, indeed, she may, it is true, lay aside shoes that are too small and clothes that are too tight, she will, on the other hand, find a whole new set of rules and regulations to live by, and regulations that are not self-imposed, but imposed by custom and enforced by the younger generation. There she will find waiting for her an ideal of what she should be herself — the ideal which was attained by Eleanor's poor grandmother; a graceful, shadowy person, sitting, her feet on a hassock, like Whistler's mother; some one who has none of the impulses of youth, which, in a grandmother, the younger generation finds so disconcerting. Even the costume of this ideal is decided upon by our exacting young people. She shall wear, our ideal grandmother, soft black or gray draperies, a piece of beautiful old lace at her neck, or a white fichu of rare old-fashioned workmanship crossed on her bosom. Caps are no longer the fashion, but our custom-ridden children regret them.

For myself, should I live to be ninety, I hope I shall fall short of this ideal in all respects. I do not wish to become a mere ornamental nonentity about whom people shall say, "What a sweet old lady!" I hope that I shall keep my family alert over my misdeeds until my end, for then I shall be sure that I shall not have slipped altogether among the shadows before I go.

Think what the ideal of old age that seems so beautiful implies; it means that the body has so lost its resiliency that the wholesome desire for action has passed, that one's own life and actions have ceased to have an interest for one, and that instead of having to snatch time to play with one's grandchildren, one has nothing to do but wait, nothing in the world to do but "be there." It is too great a price to pay for conforming to an ideal whose greatest value, after all, lies in a certain picturesqueness. I do not think, either, that any middle-aged woman would consciously choose to have her own mother one of these ideal grandmothers, although there are ways in which each one of our daughters would be glad to have us conform to an ideal of elderly conduct a little more closely.

There are daughters who, like my own, limit the field of their mothers' activities, believing firmly that they are doing so in the interest of their mothers' health. There are a great many other middle-aged women whom I see about me who constantly curtail their mothers' personal liberties, because these old ladies wish to do things which, if you please, shock the fastidious daughters in what they think is fitting for the aged. These young women know so definitely what an older woman may and may not say and do and wear!

"Mediæval" is a word I hear often nowadays on the lips of the young people. So-and-So has "mediæval" ideas on the subject of divorce or what-not. All older people are supposed to hold "mediæval" ideas, and when it turns out that one of us happens to have read and digested a new economic theory or some new book of vital interest, it is always an irritating moment to me when a younger woman remarks, in a patronizing way, "Why, how Mrs. So-and-So keeps up with the times!" But there is no reactionary older woman I know who holds as "mediæval" opinions as those which the ordinary younger women have about the older generation. The broadest-minded women I know are as tradition-bound as possible when it comes to what we older women may do.

Many an older woman, for instance, finds a style which especially suits her — a style which does not conform to the costume in which the poetical imagination pictures the dwellers in the Land of Old Age. I had an old friend who happened to fancy, as accessories to a costume in which to pass her declining years, a bustle and a certain false front. Bustles went their way, and a few people still clung to them; then even the faithful gave them up, but my friend still wore hers valiantly. It suited her so to do — and why not? Hadn't she followed the fashions long enough? Hadn't she earned her right to wear what she chose? That was the way she looked at it. She was a valiant, high-spirited old lady, full of good-tempered anecdotes about every one you ever heard of, fond

Elderly Woman

of all the bright things of life — young people, dance music, company, and bright colors; the last she wore unflinchingly. So gayly indeed and gladly did she walk up the road of time that she died, advanced in years, without old age having seemingly laid a finger on her blithe spirit. If the young people had a quiet smile at the expense of her bustle, it was a tender one. The false front which she wore with great art-lessness was an ornament to her personality. None who loved her, and they were many, would have had her altered in any respect. There was but one exception to this — her widowed daughter, who with her little girls made her home with her mother. The bustle and false front caused her the keenest pain. I do not believe my friend ever got herself ready for a "party" without the daughter trying to de-crease the size of that bustle. She never gave up trying. I remember waiting for my friend and hearing in the hall above me the sounds of ar-gument, and at last from the stairs my friend's voice: "For the hundredth time, Emily, I will *not* go out looking like a pancake! I tell you I shouldn't feel decent!"

She came into the room, her flowing silk rustling and creaking, her bonnet brave with colors, and I couldn't, as I looked at her, understand how any daughter, however hide-bound, could have wished to alter a hem's breadth of her high-hearted, courageous costume. My friend loved every one to be happy and contented around her, and I often think how many small annoyances she might have been spared had her daughter not had such firm convictions concerning the conventional dress of age. I am glad to relate, however, that my old friend wore her bustle, her daughter notwithstanding, almost to her dying day. I hope they buried it with her — she made a brave fight for it. She is to me an inspiring memory. When my children try — oh, very gently — to take from me some little habit or some peculiarity of dress, I think of her and smilingly hold on to my own, for I will not encourage them in their stupid and "mediæval" idea of the fitness of things. I will not, at my time of life, have my individuality pruned and clipped. In the matter of dress there are endless limitations for us older people. All the lighter colors are supposed to be unsuitable for us; and so for some of us they are from an æsthetic point of view, though I have known many a middle-aged woman and many a pink-cheeked, snowy-haired grandmother to whom pale pink would have been every bit as becoming as the pale lavender which custom permits.

I know one sweet old lady who has always loved pink as a favorite color. She confessed to me that it was a cross to her when she grew too old to wear it.

"Well, why don't you anyway?" I asked her, knowing very well why. *I* would not have the courage to blossom out in so much as one daring pink ribbon, but, "Why don't you?" said I.

"I do," she replied mysteriously, "I do."

I looked at her simple black gown.

"Oh, not on the *out*side! But," said she, lowering her voice, "I always run in plenty of pink ribbon in my things and I have pink ribbon garters!" she concluded triumphantly.

And only an older woman who has been cut off by an arbitrary custom from many of the pretty gay things of life will understand what a comfort those pink ribbon garters were to her.

One of my friends has already reached the

age of eighty without her interest in life being in any degree abated, and, what is far rarer, without her desire to be up and doing being in any degree diminished by age's infirmities. She has, perhaps, a more transparent look than she had some fifteen years ago, but she is still as erect as a girl. Except for looks, for her beautiful white hair and her old-lady dresses, — she happens to be one who takes kindly to the wearing of lace fichus, she is everything that conventionally an older woman should not be. You do not find her "there," not she; and not only is she not there, but she doesn't tell her daughters where she is going. They are between Margaret's age and mine, and discuss "Mother's" wild, headstrong ways in my presence. She gives them a great deal of trouble and anxiety, and it isn't all by any means simple worry for fear she may do herself some harm or over-tax her strength. She keeps a life of her own. Since her daughters have in the natural order of things assumed the helm, she has interested herself in various intellectual pursuits; she attends lectures not only here, but in the surrounding towns. She is valiant in the field of missionary labor. As her daughter sighs: "It seems to me we never send out cards for *anything* that mother doesn't take that time for getting up barrels for the Indians!" You see, her activities interfere with the family, and they will neither let her go her way unmolested nor will they accept her activity without protest. She is, and partly because of these arbitrary conventionalities, a great care to her daughters.

One of them came in the other day sighing:

"Well, I've got to go with mother to Elenwood to hear that man lecture on 'Labor Conditions' today. I *don't* see where I'm to find time."

"Your mother couldn't go alone, I suppose?" I asked tentatively.

"She could," replied this poor daughter, "for she's to meet friends at the other end, but it *looks* so bad for a woman of mother's age to go around the country alone. As if her children cared nothing for her!"

It would be a great relief to them all if this

active old lady would stay at home more. I am glad she doesn't. My high-spirited friend is one of those who are helping to kill out the conventions which are troublesome weeds in the Land of Old Age.

Other People's
Medicine

Another convention that shackles the lives of most older women is the methods which their grown children employ to conserve their elders' health. Each family has its own particular fetish as to what "Mother" ought to do for her health; almost all older women who have their children living with them have to submit themselves to the hygienic fads of their sons and daughters. In my own case it is carriages; they are the bane of my life. I could keep an accurate record of how years are crowding on me by the way my children send me around instead of letting me walk. When Margaret begins, "Colds are terribly prevalent at this time of year. Have you heard, Dudley, that Mrs. Sears has got pneumonia?" Then I know that she wants me to drive to the reception or wherever I am going.

To any one who has not passed from middle age into the place where people live who are already counted old, it may seem a far cry between Mrs. Sears's pneumonia and my having a carriage on a sunny fall day, but those who are living in that country where older people dwell will understand. To listen to our children talk to us, you might think that all we older people might live a thousand years if we only did all the tiresome, unpleasant things for our health that our children want us to do, and I suppose that I ought to be glad that my Margaret has a mania for carriages. That is the word for it — a mania. At the slightest excuse I am driven in a jolting, germ-laden, livery stable hack to and from the reception, concert, or lecture or church. This procedure has saved me, according to Margaret, all the diseases and ailments of mankind except perhaps the bubonic plague, and if that disease were prevalent in our neighborhood, I dare say Margaret would find means of proving a carriage had saved me that.

Still, there are friends of mine whose daughters have so much more unpleasant ways of preserving their mothers' lives, that I should be glad that it is nothing worse than hacks.

My friend, Mrs. Wellington, for instance, is taken out and walked and walked about until she almost drops, because her children believe that people get old and stiff because they don't walk enough. As if it wasn't because they are stiff in their joints that makes them want to keep quiet!

Mrs. Granger is dreadfully afraid she will have to give up breakfast, which is a meal she has always especially enjoyed, just to keep peace. Every little turn of any kind that she has, her children put down to her liking for griddle-cakes and syrup in the morning, since they have gone in for the no-breakfast fad. She says that every time she eats a good comfortable breakfast, the family sit around with faces as long as her arm, and she is just on the point of giving in, although she knows it will be bad for her.

Mothers cannot bear to see their children worried and distressed, and it is here that we are as much at our children's mercy as we were when they were little things at our knee and could always get around us with tears welling to the eyes and quivering upper lip.

When Margaret spoke last about a carriage, she had a little worried expression on her brow that was so like Margaret when she was two years old that I would go to church in a haywagon to please her. I never could bear to see that little puzzled, distressed look on her face. So I submitted with fairly good grace to the proposition that I should go to Mrs. Carter's reception in the hack. I made a little protest, however, because, unless I did that, I should soon lose the use of my legs altogether and perhaps degenerate into a person who has to be pushed around in a wheel chair before I am much older. I said:

"Well, Margaret, I will go to-day just to please you, but the next time I am going to use my own judgment about it. I have been going in a carriage all summer to avoid sunstroke and apoplexy, and now that fall has come, I must avoid pneumonia and tonsillitis, and in the winter I shall be avoiding slipping on the ice; but there's got to be some cranny in the year when I can go to places on my own two feet."

But while I will submit to carriages, I will not submit to everything, and I draw the line at a trained nurse every time I am a little ill. Recently I sent one of them flying, and while I might have made the scene easier for every one, still it did me good to get rid of that woman in the summary way I did — or, rather, made Margaret do; for this was one of the occasions when I shirked and took advantage of one of the privileges age gives us. Indeed, I went so far as to tell Margaret that the trained nurse or I would leave the house.

Of course, when I am really ill and prostrate, and have to be watched at night, then I am willing to have all the discomforts — to say nothing of the needless expense — of having such a woman about. But when I am well, or pretty nearly well, to have a capped and aproned and uniformed woman, with a strong, dominant will, following my every footstep and bringing me unpalatable things to eat every two hours — why then, I shall always rebel, as I have done this time.

I said to Margaret: "This illness has been a trying one to me in every respect. I have never had to keep in my bed any longer than a morning at a time since you were born. I have lain in bed now six days; three of these days I might as well have been up."

At which Margaret replied: "I am sure you are better for the rest, darling."

I know I'm not. The reason I know this is that the last three days, whenever the nurse and Margaret left me alone to go down and get some unpleasant eatable from the kitchen for me, I got up and sat in my rocker at the window, which rested my back, though I hated to hurry back to bed, as of course I had to do whenever I heard them coming. So I might just as well, as you can see for yourself, have been up and dressed all the time, without having the nervous strain of listening for their return.

Then, too, the first day I was ill, I dressed and went downstairs. Everybody made a great outcry, and they sent for the doctor again, for the sole purpose of making me do as they said.

Elderly Woman

He is a very sensible young man, and I approve of a great many of his ideas, but at the same time, like most of the modern school, he carries much too far the modern theory of keeping a person in bed until his muscles grow weak and his back aches, though, of course, he is not nearly so unreasonable about this as my own children.

"I'd like to ask you a simple question, Doctor," I said to him when he told me that, as long as my temperature was above normal, I would have to stay in bed. "How do all the working-men do — all the people with livings to earn — when their temperatures go to 102?"

He pretended, when they have a fever, that even workingmen have to stay at home first or last; but I don't believe it. When people have to earn a living, nothing will convince me that they pop thermometers down their throats every time their stomachs get upset.

What neither the doctor nor my children understand is that I know more about matters concerning my own health than any one else. During my long life I have, of course, had my ups and downs of health like other people, and with the advancing of years, especially the last three, my strength and endurance have lessened perceptibly, and I, like other middle-aged people, have had to give myself care, so I have learned pretty well what things to avoid and how to treat my own idiosyncrasies.

During this illness, how I longed for some of those old, easy-going days, when, even though I didn't feel well, I managed to get downstairs and sit quietly around with my book or even have a whiff of fresh air; and how I longed for the days when I lay down or sat up as I felt inclined, instead of lying rigid and aching in my bed, watched like a cat by a strange woman from morning till night and from night till morning. How I disliked that cot put up in my bedroom for her to sleep in!

And this was not the worst of it. It seemed to me as if that woman deliberately hid all my things. One would think, for instance, that, having made a painful attempt to do my hair — and she almost pulled out the few remaining strands that are left me, and with which I am naturally unwilling to part — it would have occurred to her to replace the brush and comb and other articles where she found them. When I slipped out of my bed to do my own hair in a comfortable way, I could find nothing whatever to do it with; all my toilet articles, which ordinarily I could have put my hand on in the dark, had disappeared. I looked all over the room for them; they had vanished utterly as if she had swallowed them. I wandered up and down, trying to find them, and, I will confess, so vexed that I hadn't any ears for Margaret's approach. When she came into the room and found me up, she exasperated me still more by saying, "Why, darling, how did you happen to be up? Why didn't you let the trained nurse get whatever you wanted?"

"Margaret" I said, "keep that woman out of here for fifteen minutes, because I don't want to say anything that I shall be sorry for later. I suppose she does what she conceives to be her duty, but a more disorderly and ill-trained woman it hasn't been my lot to meet. Where's my toothbrush? Where are my brush and comb? What has she done with my licorice tablets? And I can tell you frankly that if she has touched my pen and paper — even though I don't want them now — I shall have to tell her what I think of her. Be so kind as to find my brush and comb so that I can do my hair with some comfort. Trained nurses ought to be taught not to do one's hair up in wads and make them feel like English walnuts to lie on!"

I don't pretend that this was a gracious speech, and it is not the way that I usually feel or talk to any one, especially to my daughter. I merely quote myself to show to what a state of exasperation a woman of my age and training may be driven. That woman was there to take care of my health; the reason I suffered her about me at all was to save my family anxiety. But it is extremely trying for a woman of my years, except in cases of the most dire necessity, to have fussing about her person an outsider who upsets all her little personal ways; meddles with her personal belongings, and renders her far more uncomfortable than comfortable. I am sure that my temperature remained above normal partly through the continual irritation that I suffered because of these things.

Then, too, I know it was not good for me to have to watch every chance to slip out of

Elderly Woman

bed to brush my own teeth. Brushing my teeth in bed, or, worse still, allowing some one else to brush them for me, is a thing which I should have to be far sicker than I have ever been to have happen to me. When I give up getting out of bed to brush my teeth of my own accord, then my children may know I'm really ill, and can send, if they like, for a day nurse and a night nurse, for I shall be past caring how many troublesome and disorderly women I have about me.

Three times in one night she got up to ask me if I spoke, or if I wanted anything, just because I cleared my throat as it's my habit to do. Finally I said to her: "Miss Jenkins, if you came to my bedside less often, my chances of going to sleep would, I think, be greater, and I'm sure it is better for your health as well as mine for you to remain in your own bed."

All of which shows under what a nervous pressure I have been forced to live. I explained my point of view to Margaret after the departure of the nurse. I said to my daughter: "Margaret, I'm taking five kinds of pills and tonics, and as I've lived with my own stomach now a large number of years, I am perfectly sure that the reason why my appetite remains so poor is that I'm constantly dosing, and you need bring me no more of those strychnine tablets and you can put the pepsin away, and as for the liquid things in bottles, I won't take them either."

I stuck to this for quite a little while, but Margaret had got it into her head that my whole life and existence depended on a few little pasteboard boxes of pills. Lines that I don't remember having seen in her face since Betty was so ill appeared there. Finally, she came to my bedside and took my hand and said: "Mother, I simply can't bear to see you trifling with your health in this way, and I don't think it's fair to us to do as you are doing. You can't get well, and you can't get strong, unless you will take care of yourself."

Her tone and her whole manner touched me, and I saw what people who live in the Land of Old Age sometimes forget how great and pressing the things we know to be of little importance seem to our great, grown-up sons and daughters. There was in Margaret's tone and in her attitude almost that poignant agony that a mother has over her sick child.

She could not bear to have me sick. I saw then that each meal that I could not eat, each time I did not take my medicine — even my just rebellion against my trained nurse — had taken from her a little of her strength and vitality.

It is hard, when one is ill and suffering one's self, to realize the extent to which this reacts on those about us, especially for us older people. I had a quick vision of Margaret's seeing me walking off wantonly, needlessly, into the land of shadows. I know, of course, that when the day comes, pills and trained nurses and gruel will not retard my footsteps, and I shall very much like to pass through the series of minor illnesses that may be before me in my own way, comfortably, without too much nagging and without having my hair-brushes hidden, or having to lie in bed when I know it is bad for my back. But after all, I think I saw on that morning that my annoyances had been small compared to Margaret's anxieties. She threw aside for the moment the smiling "You-will-be-better-to-morrow" mask that she has consistently assumed from the beginning of my illness, and I realized for the first time that the week had been one where shadowy fears had pressed about her, taking from her her gaiety, her confidence. Each time I had sprung from my bed to get something I wanted, she had seen the shadows about me; each moment of my weakness had whispered desolation to her.

I thought of the long evenings that she and Dudley had passed together, discussing with the trained nurse my shortcomings and my willfulnesses; and I saw that my small rebellions had been to her not small rebellions at all, but willful throwing away of so many of the days that it may be yet permitted us to pass together.

For one moment I was almost sorry that I had sent that woman away, but that moment of weakness did not stay long, because, after all, it's I who will have to be the judge of how to lengthen out the span of those days. At the same time, as we sat there together in silence, Margaret holding my hand and I looking at the anxious lines in her face, I made up my mind to take the pepsin and the strychnine and all the other things that they make such a fuss over.

So I told Margaret when she implored (and I can't translate to you her accent of anxiety), "Now do take the medicine the doctor left for you; it certainly will strengthen you," — "I will, Margaret."

But even then a flicker of spirit rose in me; for all of Margaret's and Dudley's agonizing, I'm not dead yet — very far from it — and it's very seldom that I get a good chance to influence my children's lives. So that is why I said to my daughter:

"Margaret, I can see that you are very anxious about me. But I'm equally anxious about you, though I don't presume to nag you and make such a fuss about it. I will take the tablets and the tonics and the powders, and even the horrid things put up in gelatine capsules, which are as hard to swallow as any hen's egg in its shell, if you will make a few concessions on your part: that heavy tailored skirt that you've been wearing I know is the cause of your backache. Will you promise me to put it aside, for a while anyway?"

"Yes, mother," Margaret agreed.

"And will you try to eat your meals more regularly?" (For Margaret has been doing a great deal of outside club work, and half the time comes home to lunch ten to fifteen minutes late, when all the meat is cold and spoiled, and I know that it will injure her stomach in the long run.)

"Margaret," I said, "I've studied the rules of health for a great many years, and as you are fond of boasting, I'm in pretty good condition as a rule, considering my time of life and the things I've been through. So if I'm to do what you want me to, I think it is only fair that you should, in smaller matters, be guided by me a little bit; and this sitting and reading so far from the light and spoiling your eyes is a thing that has got to be put a stop to, if I am to take another strychnine tablet."

Margaret agreed readily to all these things. It may seem to you that I was taking an unfair advantage; but I do my share of silent worrying on my own side, and it seemed to me only fair exchange, because undoubtedly it will benefit my health to be saved these small anxieties, besides benefiting Margaret's.

Margaret agreed readily because I think she saw the reasonableness and justice of my remarks.

"May I bring you tapioca now?" she asked at the end of my talk.

"No, Margaret," I replied. "I am going down to dinner to-day, and I am going to eat some solid food — things that I *want* to eat, which I know will be much better for my health."

The Compensations
of Age

I grumble a good deal, it seems to me, about my children's too anxious care of me; I make life seem shorn of many of its pleasures — and so it is; but age also clips life of complications. It is the great simplifier.

For instance, the moment my eye fell upon my new neighbors, I knew I wasn't going to like them. This may sound as though I am disagreeable and ill-natured, but I don't think I am. Indeed I have lived so long in this world that I feel free to express my opinions without being afraid of being misunderstood. A younger woman might not give out so frankly what she thinks, as she has her reputation to make; but one opinion, more or less, of my neighbors, will not alter my reputation, for if I have proved myself, in the long time I have stayed in this world, kindly and not hard to please and ready to make allowances, I believe people will make allowances for me, and it will not hurt me one bit to ease my mind by saying that I do not fancy my new neighbors. I don't suppose I had any reason for it, for they seemed very nice and pleasant people.

The older woman, the one Margaret picked out as a companion for me, was fastened into one of those new-fangled frocks that have hooks in every conceivable spot where a hook ought not to be and none where they ought to be. Not that this had anything to do with my liking her, as I have plenty of friends of my own age who enjoy keeping up with the styles and like to have the dressing hour one of martyr-dom. I just didn't feel that these people and I would have anything to talk about, and conver-sation would always be of that rudimentary kind that happens on the outskirts of acquain-tance.

I said nothing about this, however, and in a few days, when Margaret suggested we should call, "It seems," said I, "rather damp to me to-day. You run over, Margaret dear, so as to be nice and cordial and leave my cards. If we are in for a spell of bad weather, I may not get around for a week or two."

So saying, I settled myself comfortably in my chair and told the maid to telephone to my friend Mrs. Wellington to see if she would come and play logomachy. I sat there waiting with that most comfortable of all feelings in my heart — a feeling that comes of having decently avoided a disagreeable duty. I looked back over my long life and thought of the many times I had called and called and called on people I didn't want to — new church people who I thought were lonely; people who were friends of friends of mine with whom I had no more in common than I had with a flagstaff.

Before she went out, Margaret asked, "Are there any more calls you don't feel like making? for I might as well do them all up, now that I am started."

At that I made out a list of all the people I

didn't especially want to see in town. It was not a very large one, for I am fond of my fellow creatures. Though, strictly speaking, my day of calling is over, when I want to see any one I go and see them and spend a good hour or more in a real talk. I am no longer a young woman; I am an elderly woman, and will soon be old, and the day for me, thank goodness, is past when I spend an afternoon in that most senseless occupation — fifteen minute calls, where the people are called upon according to neighborhood, and not because any one feels any particular need of their conversation.

In many ways, as we advance in years, we return to the attitude we had when we were children. If we grow old wisely, we lay aside the senseless forms and meaningless conventions of society and go back to a more primitive mode of social intercourse, picking our friends the way children do — because we like them — spending time enough with them to get some real good out of them.

It was with joy that I saw my daughter depart to call upon the Towners, for this was the name of the new people. In this world, of course Towners have to be called upon, but oh, glorious day! the time is past when it is I who must do it. If I have to forego some things I would like to do; if old age in the shape of waning strength says to me often, "Thou shalt not!" so do my years smile upon me and say to me, "Thou needst not."

I have moments of unhappiness and rebellion, as I suppose most older women have as old age creeps on them unawares as they work and dream and live; I have moments of sorrow that my real work in the world is done, and moments of sadness that my children no longer come to me, but spare me, not wishing to trouble me; but oh, with what happiness do I leave the performing of some duties to the younger generation. Think what an emancipation it would be if some voice should cry, "No more calls!" This is what the voice of age said to me, as I sat that afternoon by the window watching my dear daughter ply dutifully forth. Many years will have to pass by before she can sit down quietly before her pleasant open fire and rejoice that never, never again will she need to make a duty call.

Elderly Woman

As I watched Margaret go her way on her round of calls, I saw all the family of tiresome duties before me, not only calls, but committee meetings of one kind and another. Not a committee meeting do I have to go to. I don't have to feel like a beggar getting money for the church organ or the new church carpet. I did these things willingly and cheerfully in my time, and now, thank goodness, I don't have to do them. I even make the confession that there are some times, when Margaret says to me, "Mother, it's too rainy for you to go to church," that I agree with her with a certain alacrity.

Oh, blessed are the immunities of age!

This morning there walked past my house a young person. She was pretty, she was young. I have no doubt that I should have been an object of pity in her eyes as I sat there in my comfortable wide chair in my comfortable dress, which, if you please, is a waist and skirt, the waist hooking in the front. This pretty young person's back hair was built out one foot behind her head with what aids I am too innocent to pretend to tell you; her frock was of the kind that fits with distressing closeness until it bursts out in a flare of pleats at the knees, and she wore upon her head a prodigious hat. Her type was not extreme. I see young women and maidens every day more fantastically and uncomfortably arrayed.

"Oh," I thought to myself, "there's a spring in youth, to be sure, and a joyousness in it, but oh, how uncomfortable youth makes itself!"

I see my daughter Margaret clawing around her spinal column, trying to hook her clothes up the back, and rejoice that I am of an age where, fashion book or no fashion book, things may yet fasten up the front. I don't need to wear a hat that looks like a chimney or a monstrous mushroom; I can wear broad, low-heeled, cloth-topped shoes while the styles in shoes skip around from heavy mannish to paper soles and pointed toes.

There are women, of course, who do not take advantage of the blessed privileges which age brings them, but, after all, not many of us. Most of us have sense given us to realize that there are certain fads in this world that we are through with.

So I confess that I saw the little girl with

the imposing hair and hat go her way without envying her her youth. Would I not like to be young again? Who would not if they could have youth plus the wisdom which their years have given them?

It may be that it is "sour grapes" that makes me feel as I do, but a profound thankfulness sweeps over me when I run through the long list of things I need not do any more, and if I rejoice that certain distasteful duties are removed from me, how much more do I rejoice over the amusements that did not amuse me that I no longer have to go to. No more do I have to attend concerts of an ultra-classical nature; no longer do I have to read the newest book if I do not choose to; if I am ever bored, it is not any longer by those things which are supposed to divert me.

Fancy your life stripped of all the things that are tiresome to do, that are a weariness to your spirit. What does all this cry about the simple life mean, this turning to nature, this camping in Maine woods, this flying to little shacks by the seashore? Not so much the desire for beauty, for that is accessible to very many people, but leisure to enjoy it, and attaining this leisure by throwing out of the window what one might call "the padding of life." I do not have to leave my comfortable home for an uncomfortable, half-furnished shanty to revel in the beauty of the maple tree which makes a golden glory outside my window. Without effort on my part life has handed me these extra hours in which to look around the world and enjoy the beauties of it with peace in my heart, and it seems that for those who look upon age rightly, life becomes a spacious, roomy place. For some the spaciousness means loneliness; through the vaulted roominess of the days voices echo infrequently; the wide vistas of time are unpeopled and bare; memories only walk through — shadowy and with sad eyes. I can only thank God that age has not come to me in such a guise. For me and many of my contemporaries the priceless gift of time has been the recompense of our having lived so long in this world; and instead of our days being full of the needful but distasteful duties, and cluttered, besides, and choked with the pleasureless pleasurings in which I see those younger than myself spending their days, we may now turn and do the things which we have always wanted to do. And for those who have lived with zest and vigor — that is to say, those who have lived at all — there is hardly one who has not had some pursuit or some taste which was crowded out of their lives. If you look around the world you may see any number of vigorous elderly women doing the things they wanted to do all their days, and doing them with the earnestness and relish of children at play.

The Spending
of Time

There are some older people to whom life has not handed out so many vacant spaces, and whose days yet remain crowded, not with the unavoidable duties, but with those that others impose upon them.

I know a valiant old lady of seventy whose vigorous and sane presence was of such inspiration to her many daughters that "mother" was on a perpetual round of visits of advice and consolation. As is the case with so dominant and self-reliant a nature, she had raised up a brood of fine women, but women accustomed to rely upon her, even into middle age. As happens often in such cases, she first domineered over them and they in turn ate up her time and her leisure until she rebelled against this tender slavery of her own creating. One day she arose, saying, "Before another of these granddaughters of mine gets the croup, I'm going around the world!" — which, it seems, she had always desired to do, but had not had the time for. So, with much dexterity, she eluded the vigilance of her loving children, hopped upon a boat, and informed them by telegram where she was going.

"For," she told me by letter, "I have no intention of viewing the marvels of this earth with a rhinitis pill popped into my mouth by one of my daughters every few minutes. I don't want to go through the tombs of the Ptolemies with galoshes on my feet, as I know I should have to do if one of the girls went with me."

In one's travels around the earth one meets many elderly people who, like this friend of mine, are seeing at last the sights they had planned to see all their days; fulfilling the dreams, often-times, of a far remote youth.

Again, it is some desire for knowledge that

we indulge in in our old age. Two old friends of mine — a retired minister and his wife — are at this moment pursuing the study of biology with all the ardor of youth. Through the years of his long life this dear man and his wife had looked forward to the time when they might slake their curiosity about the wonders of the earth, and now they are doing it with the passion of youth. It was a real need with them and a true desire which they had always between them kept alive. I do not know any reward that a life of toil can hold more precious than this fulfillment of a lifelong desire.

Another friend of mine had a very full life, though she never married. She took care of her brother's house — a complicated establishment full of guests; but always she cherished a love for the Romance languages and read much of their literature in translation; and when she had time, which was after her sixty-fifth birthday, she learned Spanish and French and Italian.

At this minute, down the street Mrs. Baker is making rugs and carpets out of all the rags she has saved for the last thirty years. The story of how she has conserved these pieces is an epic, a tribute to the force and persistence of the human will. Her children, one and all, have tried to make her throw away "all that rubbish." They have pointed out to her that her collection of old pieces was a mania, and that nothing would ever come of it; also, they might be doing "somebody some good." During her absence her daughters would lead commiserating friends to the attic and show them rag-bags bursting, trunks overflowing, bureau drawers yawning, with the pieces their mother had collected. Oh, the younger and older generations had some doughty passages-at-arms over what the younger women called a "needless and unhygienic accumulation."

"Some day," Mrs. Baker persisted, "I intend to make rag carpets from them — when I have time."

She has time now, and, I am glad to say, is doing what she always wanted to. The making of rag carpets may not have been a high goal to aim at, but what matter? The longer I live, the more I believe it is the spirit in which we do things that makes our acts pleasing or displeasing to a Greater Intelligence. Who knows whether rag carpets made with a cheerfulness which is in itself a prayer may not be more pleasing to the Lord than much more pretentious occupations performed sadly?

To many of us the moment of leisure comes too late; we allow the daily occupations of our business to crowd upon us so in middle life that, when old age comes upon us, it finds us without resource. So it is with men, while women fill up the depths of the spirit with a countless reiteration of detail, bankrupting themselves; leaving themselves dependent upon the good will of others for all amusement.

Many of us have worked so hard and life has treated us so ungently that all the fair lights that burned for us in the country of youth have been put out; but, thank God! it isn't so with all. That elusive moment, "when I have time," that every one talks about, comes to almost all of us, and it finds a certain number of us with a will to do what we like. But here with the things that we want to do, we often find ourselves in the position of children who plan out tasks that their little strength will not perform. For ever and ever we bruise ourselves against the limitations of the flesh. Oh, the books that we wish to read, for which our eyes do not serve; the pleasurings denied us; the work cut away from us because of the limitation of our strength, and the knowledge that this limitation must always increase. The size of the earth over which one may roam shrinks day by day, until it decreases to the house, to one's room, to one's bed; and finally to the narrowest space of all.

So side by side with the things that we can now do because we have more time are the things that we have no strength for and the things that our children promise to do for us and never get around to — our children who are so eager to perform all sorts of small kindnesses.

I know that I have been wanting for three years to straighten my attic the way I would like to see it done, and neither have I been permitted to do it, nor will my children do it for me. It is one of those things that has got to be done by one of the family; no cleaning-woman can do anything except the heavier part of the work. And now, whenever I go up and sort over a trunk of letters or a chest of drawers, some one is sure to hear me walking around up there and come after me, until what Margaret and Dudley call my "attic face" is a joke in the family. They pretend that there is a certain joyful but furtive look comes over me when I have "designs," as Dudley says, on the attic.

"That attic, I hope, will never get cleared," he tells me. "It is all the joy to you that a double life would be. It gives you the joy of forbidden fruit. As long as it isn't cleared, you can sneak up there and go on a terrible debauch; of course you are generally ill and miserable after it, but who minds that when they have made a night of it?"

In this disrespectful way does my son joke me, not realizing that the state of the attic is a real source of annoyance to me.

Almost every older woman has something equivalent to my attic. Oftentimes this attic is a thing a woman is strong enough to do herself, but which her children, with their too loving care, prevent her doing. Sometimes little household duties that she has attended to all her life herself, from one day to another, her children have decided she isn't strong enough to do.

Elderly Woman

Perhaps one time she got tired; who doesn't? Young people as well as old get tired. And sometimes I think that those old people are most to be envied, after all, who keep forever in the harness and to whom each day brings its compulsory duties; in them lies the essence of youth, which, after all, I suppose, has a good deal to do with the feeling that one is helping to make the wheels of the world's work go round.

I think that many a woman has had her life shortened by this fretting that might have been avoided, much more than it would have been by the fatigue that doing what she wished to would incur. When day after day one asks those young people, upon whom one has become dependent for some service, to look after this or that, the chains of age weigh heavily. We have to ask in all the varying tones that the dependent must use, from the cajolery with which we get our own way to the futile bursts of irritation, and in the end perhaps resort to subconscious strategy, lucky at last if we can but accomplish our purpose. When I do this there is a feeling deep in my heart of how roundabout, how circuitous, are my acts, how unlike the "I" that once brought about the small things in the world that I wished to; so short a time ago I could accomplish in my life, in the ordering of my household, what I wished.

The spaces in our lives that our children have helped to empty by making it difficult for us to do those things which they consider harmful for our well-being, they try to fill up with their kindly and blundering hands. Every older woman who lives much with her children knows what I mean.

Margaret and Dudley, I know, feel that I don't see enough of women of my own age. Mrs. Allen, at the other end of the town, and I have a very good time together whenever we meet, and yet it is quite a distance — for although it is a little town where we live, it is sprawled all along the Common — for us on our old legs to run in and out, and we have managed to live half a life-time without ever becoming intimate, notwithstanding a very real enjoyment we have in each other's society.

This liking Dudley tries to further as though it was a hothouse plant.

Elderly Woman

"You look 'down,' mother; shan't I telephone to Mrs. Allen? Or let me run down in the motor and get her for you." Or, "I'm just going over to Lembury; shan't I drop you at Mrs. Allen's for a half-hour?" until Mrs. Allen has become to me the symbol of "amusing mother."

When I see them at it, it touches me in my heart and it touches me in my temper as well. I don't want to be amused; I don't want to have occupation found for me. If I have nothing better to do than to sit with my hands folded, then I prefer to sit; nor does conversation like this affect me in the slightest.

Margaret will say to Dudley:

"I think that Mrs. So-and-So has changed very much this last year. She has allowed herself to lose interest in things."

"Yes," Dudley will reply, "I think an older woman makes a great mistake not to cultivate her own hobbies."

"And beside that," Margaret will add, "keep abreast with the times. Now there is Mrs. Griscom," she went on in reproving tones, "I see her out motoring with her son almost every day."

Now here I knew what they were getting to; they wanted me to go out in Dudley's new motor. Now, if there's anything I dislike it is nasty, smelly, jouncing, child-grazing, dog-smashing, chicken-routing motors. I ride along with my heart in my mouth, not for my own life and limbs, although those are uncomfortable enough being jounced along like a piece of corn in a popper, which seems to me no way for a woman to spend her few remaining years of life; but it is for the people along the way-side whom we almost crush — the trembling horses, the squawking hens, the frightened children that rack my nerves.

I don't like motors any more than I like trolley cars, although I ride in the cars when I have to go from one town to another, but I don't enjoy them any more than I enjoy trains. If all my neighbors want to do it and enjoy it, let them — I don't intend to! But Margaret always had a mania for having me ride; before Dudley got the car, it was carriages, but now, under one pretext or another, they try to get me to go motoring with Dudley. They say that if I once get into the car I will get to like it, but

Elderly Woman

I know that I shall not. I shall not get to like it any more than I shall ever have Mrs. Allen for my bosom friend.

These things can't be forced upon one; we will for ever and ever, young or old, choose our amusement from some hidden spring within ourselves, and if new doors are to be opened to us of enjoyment, it is our hands that must lift the latch, though we follow in the lead of some beloved person.

The Land of Old Age

I have talked, I suppose, rather fancifully about what I have chosen to call the Land of Old Age. It is because old age has seemed to me often not only a state of mind, or a physical condition, but a sort of different dimension, an actual country where we who are older must live. Often I see people approaching its boundaries, withdrawing from them, ignoring them, and next I know, I come across a new citizen. It is an invisible country — this Land of Old Age — and however young you are, you have been near it. I should count you unfortunate, indeed, if in the heat of the day you had not turned into its shady by-paths and lingered a moment with its quiet dwellers. It is a very peaceful land; there is not much work to be done; duty is rarely seen; so seldom, in fact, that sometimes those of us who have gone there to live for good feel that we have passed our time of usefulness, and have moments of hot resentment that we are not out in the world doing its work for it.

I feel that way myself often, and at such times make excursions outside; always the gentle hands of my children lead me back to my own country. And I sometimes feel that the reason we resist taking up our places there is this sense that we are not allowed to come out when we wish; that we are kept prisoners, not through our own weaknesses, but because there are certain conventions as to what is suitable or unsuitable for us old people.

But lately I have come to believe that the people who live in the Land of Old Age have their own appointed part to play, and that they help make up the sum of life.

After all, one need not dust and sweep and make pies and cake, to be of service to those we

love. We would not wish to see out little children fetch and carry, and yet they are the dear-
est things in the world to us. So we older
people, I believe, do more than we know for
those we love when we sit in our own quiet
country, as I found out a little while ago when I
started to make an excursion into the world
that works.

The mistake our younger people make is
in regarding age as a fixed quantity. They act on
the firm conviction that you are older every day
you live, whereas age is as relative and variable
as youth. You have only to warm the blood
with any emotion — joy or relief from suspense
or patriotism or pity — and the Land of Old
Age vanishes; especially when there is a great
calamity, the old people troop forth as eager to
lend a hand, as strong to do a day's work, as
ever they were; and I think it is not their fault
that they so often turn their disappointed faces
back to their familiar country without having
taken part in what is going on.

When I heard, for instance, that a little
town which squats dirty and hard-working on
the outskirts of our village had been flooded in

the spring freshet, and that there were twenty homeless families and a hundred and fifty people out of work, I was eager to help. Our whole town at once bestirred itself to do something, and I was glad that the Committee of Ways and Means met at our house, even if their ways of doing things seemed cumbrous to me. In my day when we gave benefits, we had no committees nor chairmen nor any other kind of machinery. One of the ladies went around with a notebook from house to house and asked what might be expected from each one, and her paper at the end of the day read: "Mrs. Smith, four dozen biscuits; Mrs. Jones, two layer-cakes," etc. Mrs. Jeremiah Curtis and Mrs. Henry Lessey always did the scalloped oysters. (How I should enjoy a plate of scalloped oysters like that for my supper to-night!) And in this easy fashion we brought the thing about.

But I was eager, just the same, to join the ladies assembled in my parlors. And now an odd thing happened. I suppose as one gets along in years one gets acquainted less readily with the new people; for here in my own village where I have lived over thirty years, and in my

own house, I found myself an outsider, sur-
rounded by people whom I barely knew by
sight. They began the meeting in the stiff, for-
mal way I believe is known as parliamentary,
but after a little while they limbered up and
began discussing the affair more naturally, and I
became interested. It came over me that something ought to be done right away for these
poor creatures. So I said:

"Ladies, this party five days off isn't going
to clothe those blessed children, or their fathers
or mothers, for that matter, who were driven
out of their homes in the night with only what
they had on them."

"Why, what a good idea!" exclaimed one
of the ladies.

Perhaps I am supersensitive, but it seemed
to me she was surprised that I at my age was capable of any ideas at all. I was about to say that
I would have a canopy-top called from the stable and make a house-to-house canvass and
have a big lot of things ready to send out by the
evening trolley, when some one said: "I move
that we appoint an Immediate Relief Commit-

tee. Can't some one ring up Susan Millsborough? She's just the one to push that through."

In spite of myself I felt a little disappointed, for it is a great satisfaction to do things for people one's self and to do them in *one's own way*. Before I spoke I have seen myself on the rounds in the canopy-top, but now I suddenly felt very much out of it again. Not only were there faces and methods of work new to me, but my own little idea was picked away from me and gobbled into their cumbrous modern machinery. There was a great deal of telephoning back and forth, and it was on my tongue a half-dozen times to offer to go; but I realized that the canopy-top and I, from whatever point of view one chose to look at us, were not a committee.

So I held my tongue — until I got interested again. It was to be, I gathered, a huge entertainment, with all sorts of elaborations. All the simple affairs, such as we would in former times have given for two years rolled into one, wouldn't have made such a great affair. I who knew the slender resources of our little town so well, for we are not a rich village, found myself saying:

"Won't the cost of getting it up take away the greater part of the profits?"

"It will be such an advertisement of the whole disaster," one of them assured me. "The other towns in the neighborhood, after our example, will feel they have to do something handsome."

There was not the least suggestion of patronage in her tone, and it was not due to her that I felt that my little remark had flown so wide of the point, but only that we talked across the gap Time had made between us, she on the one side understanding the new methods, and I understanding only those I was used to. But all the same, that afternoon I stood on my own little territory and listened to how people did things in the world, with an ever-growing sense of isolation. Many of the things in this world that are hard to bear are no one's fault at all; they are so because the world is as it is.

All the next day my daughter Margaret bounced in and out unceasingly. I tried to catch her a dozen times, for I wanted so very much to do something, however little, for the distressed people — I have always been so used to doing my share in the world. At last I buttonholed Margaret.

"Listen, Margaret," I began.

"Excuse me for a moment, darling; there's the telephone."

After a hurried conference, Margaret pinned on her hat. I followed her up.

"Before you go," I hastened to say, "let me ask you one thing."

"I've only four minutes to catch the four-thirty-two trolley," she answered, and kissed me affectionately and dashed away.

One of the children ran after her, calling:

"Mamma, may I —"

"Ask your uncle," called my daughter; and her tone and gesture, as though she couldn't stand one more thing, made me see under what pressure she was working.

At that moment my son Dudley walked up the path. I was planted on the steps where Margaret had left me when she whirled by.

"Anything I can do?" he asked.

He was hurried, too, but of all my children he is the one who always has time for me.

"All I want to know is, *do* they want me to make cake for them," I said, with some spirit, for I was tired of being put off like an importunate child. I make an excellent Hartford election-cake, and it is much better on the second or third day. My cake, indeed, is famous among my children and grandchildren, and I thought that in this way I could give my mite to the poor distressed people.

"That would be awfully nice, mother." Dudley's tone was apologetic. "But they've already arranged for the cake — the baker gives the material at wholesale prices and does the work. We wanted to pay for his time, but he says it will be a good advertisement. Not that yours wouldn't be lots better —"

"I wanted to do something for them," I said forlornly.

"Why, didn't you do enough? You know you've given more to the Immediate Relief Committee than you can afford. Isn't that enough?" He took my arm. "Here," he said," let me bring your chair into the shade. It's so pleasant here

this afternoon. I only wish I had the time —"
and Dudley was off too.

The last thing I wanted was to sit quietly
in the shade, for I am what the people around
here call "a mighty spry old lady." Just how old I
will not tell, for it was a convention of my generation that a woman ought not to be a minute
older than she could help. I am not old enough
yet, at any rate, to have taken to boasting about
the remarkable number of years I have stayed in
the world. But I am old enough for my middle-
aged sons and daughters to boast for me about
how active I am for my years, and they boast
about it as if the fair health I enjoy was some
virtue of their own. Perhaps the good care they
take of me *is* the reason for my being so well,
but down in the bottom of my heart is the conviction that, had I followed all their advice, and
led the packed-in-cotton-wool existence they
have marked out for me, and sent for the doctor
as often as they have wanted me to, I should be
a bedridden old hypochondriac at this moment
instead of being so ready and willing to do my
share of work.

I sat down obediently, however, and

picked up a magazine that was lying near by; and under pretense of reading I reviewed the last two days, quite dispassionately and soberly. I had come forth from the quiet Land of Old Age. For a moment, in the stress of interest for those poor homeless people, I had forgotten that Margaret and her Committee of Ways and Means and I were not contemporaries. I had had suggestions to give, and I had been ready and strong to lend a hand where a hand was needed. I had forgotten, I say, that I am what people call "old," and now as I sat idle in the shade I remembered, and all at once I felt rather tired and strangely aloof from the things that were going on around me.

Through no one's fault except my own I had been thwarted and my own ideals taken from me. My fault was the irreparable one of belonging to the generation of those whose business it is to sit comfortably in the shade and wait — who can say for what? Just then my little grandchild Edith came up to me, and, without asking, took my magazine from my hand to look at the pictures, and it occurred to me that those older children who had taken my work from me — without asking, either — had done it as serenely unconscious as Edith was that I might want the work for myself.

And wasn't I a still older child myself? Need I sit and sulk because the older children wouldn't let me play at their game? They could play it better without me, they didn't need me, thought I, with the best philosophy in the world — and all the time I wanted to be playing with them, for in my play I would forget a little while that I wasn't, after all, their age. I think that our dear children who look after us so well and see that we don't tire ourselves, and scold us gently when we sit in drafts — we "spry old ladies,"— forget, in the care of our ailing bodies, that it is better sometimes for the body to be tired, if the spirit isn't. It is good for us to take what part we may in the affairs of life. The Land of Old Age isn't, as our children think, just a place for people to coddle themselves in. When I got so far in my thought, two more of my grandchildren ran up to me. They had been sent home from the town hall. It seems they had been in the way.

"Well," thought I, "here we are, too old

and too young. We can play together if neither of us can play with the big children."

It came over me that perhaps it was just as well that we weren't all of us hurrying and working, and that at the day's end there should be some one not too tired. Just then there turned in at the gate a friend of mine. Though she is still in her twenties, she and I are the best of friends. Her pleasant face was lined with care, and she looked worried and tired.

"Dear child, what is the matter?" I asked.

"It's that the Daughters of the American Revolution and the Woman's Village Improvement Society each want to decorate the hall, and they're quarreling, and nothing's getting done," she said, and burst into tears.

I patted her head and wiped her tears off, and we made some iced tea, and I sent her off at least quite cheered up.

"I had to come down and get out of it for a minute. It was so nice of you to be sitting there so cool and rested," she added enviously.

Then one by one my tired, overworked children came home to me. Without knowing what they did, they turned to me for comfort and for rest, and I took care of them and smoothed out their difficulties, and laughed with them and sympathized with them. They seemed very young to me, my big children, and I realized that they turned to me as they always had, and that I still had things to give them and things to do for them. What if my body must be quiet? It seemed to me that night that I gave them their supper and put them to bed as I had done so many times when they were small, for there are blessed moments in all mothers' lives when their children seem again little children. They had come to me in the quiet land I live in to be rested, as every one in the world turns to that land of peace, as all busy, hurried workers and tired mothers turn into these still, quiet roads.

There we sit, we older men and women, waiting for our children to come to us. They find us there ready to tell them how little their little troubles mean, for in our country the perspectives are long, and we look down long vistas on the road of years. In their great troubles we can say, "I know, I understand," for we have worked and have seen all the things our children must see. And if now and then the world of work calls to us, and if for a moment we like to pretend that the details of the hour are important, let us go out at will, and play at work, for in our hearts we know that we live in the Land of Old Age.

Chapter VIII

Grandmothers and Grandchildren

The human beings that are closest to the Land of Old Age are the children. In so many ways their limitations are ours. Margaret has to apply the same "Thou shalt nots" to Betty that she does to me. For instance, I had planned to go over for a game of backgammon with an old friend of mine, Eliza Storrs, and hadn't paid much attention to the weather; neither had my little granddaughter Betty; so each of us was making her preparations briskly when Margaret nipped us both in the bud. Betty was easy enough to nip. All Margaret had to do with her was to tell her quite openly and frankly that

today was a nasty day, quite unsuitable for a little girl to be abroad in. It was a different story
with me. I was a child of a larger growth, headstrong, and hard to manage, so my daughter ap-
proached me with tact, as one must children of
my sort. She opened fire craftily in this wise:

"Wasn't it awful about poor Mrs. Allen's
hip?" said she. "I hear she isn't getting on at all."
(Mrs. Allen fell the other day on a slippery
pavement and broke her hip.) "Her daughter
begged and begged her to take a carriage, but
she wouldn't," my guileful daughter continued.
"Imagine her feelings when her mother was
brought home. They say she will always have
to walk with a crutch."

Now a great many more people of Margaret's age get hurt every year than women of
mine, but I didn't feel like arguing the point.

"It was just such a day. I suppose it's silly of
me, but every time you go out in bad weather
since then —" says Margaret, coming to the
point.

"Is it bad underfoot?" I asked.

"*Awful!*" Margaret replied fervently. "People
fairly skate along."

"I won't go, then," I decided.

I must say that while I see through Margaret's guile, I like to be given the semblance of choice, and so I suppose does the child who is hard to manage.

I heard Betty asking if she couldn't have some little girls to play with her, and Margaret answer that she doubted if other mothers would let their children out, so I called Betty up to me. In ten minutes we had both forgotten the weather and everything else; we might have been the same age, so much we enjoyed each other's society.

The front door slammed, and out popped Margaret into the leg-breaking weather.

"She won't let us go out, but she goes out herself, I notice," observed Betty, with pessimism.

I did notice, and I noticed what Betty didn't, that she and I were housebound for exactly the same reasons — since neither of us had seemed to have judgment to stay in of her own accord — Margaret, being anxious about our health, had kept us in.

Nor was this the only place that Betty and

I met on common ground; each one of us was dependent, each one of us a source of anxiety to those nearest us, each one of us ministered to with the same touching devotion. Like Betty, I had my moments of rebellion, and my efforts for liberty were as futile as hers — more futile, indeed, for each year that passed brought with it new reasons for the reasonableness of my children's tender tyranny. I suppose it is because we are so alike that the sympathy between old people and little children is as old as the world. As I sat telling stories to Betty, I could but think how, all the world over, there were grandparents rejoicing in their grandchildren, tending them, playing with them, teaching them the old baby games that go back to the beginning of time. Very often I echo in different words some observation of Betty's — the ignorance of childhood and the wisdom of age touch each other at more points than one. Many of the occupations and preoccupations of "grown people" like Margaret seem equally profitless to Betty and to me. We are both so far away from the rush of events that the passions and ambitions of the world trouble neither of us. I have forgotten about them, and Betty hasn't found them out — we are on an equal footing of indifference. Even the faults of the grandparents and grandchildren are alike; some of us are as self-centred as children, and others of us have the same naïve egotism.

There is a certain exquisite flattery in our grandchildren's company. Betty loves everything I do. I seem to her witty, accomplished, and gifted. More than this, she treats me as an equal. She is ignorant of drafts; she is not afraid all the time that I am going to tire myself out. In a word, she doesn't know that when she comes to see me she comes into the Land of Old Age. She doesn't know that it's because I am old that I have all the time there is, while her mother has to "make time" for her. For all Betty does for me I try to repay her by indulgences of all sorts — sometimes by forbidden indulgences. For these I get mildly scolded, but I keep right on. I have yet to hear of a boy who grew up a bad man because of the little indulgences his grandfather showered on him, nor of one who grew up a dyspeptic because of the surreptitious cookies his grandmother gave him. I am sure I am no worse a woman because my grandmother begged me off from some well-merited punishments. So I spoil my grand-children as much as I can, which is as much as I am let.

There was a time when I wasn't allowed to spoil them at all. I hardly knew my older grand-children as babies, for I went through, like so many other women of my generation, what I call "The Grandmother's Tragedy."

I first heard about it from Eliza Storrs. How often of late years I have had occasion to think of the morning she plumped herself down in my rocking chair. I can remember just how the corners of her pleasant mouth were drawn down, and in what a discouraged way she flapped her fan back and forth.

"It's awfully hard work learning how to be a grandmother," she complained.

"Well," thought I complacently, "if there's one thing I shan't have to learn, it's *that*. People may have to learn how to be mothers, but not how to be grandmothers."

I was very sure of my ground because I had just that minute, you might say, got to be a grandmother myself; my arms were aching for my little grandson, whom I had never seen, my oldest son's first child. I was so full of the grandmother feeling, so eager for sight of the blessed little fellow, that I couldn't believe the woman of my age existed who wasn't a ready-made, accomplished grandmother.

"It's easy enough to be the kind of grandmother *you* think you ought to, but what's hard is to be the kind of grandmother *they* want you to be," Eliza explained, flapping her fan mournfully.

I hadn't the least idea then what Eliza was talking about, so I wasn't a bit sympathetic. I wanted, indeed, to laugh, she looked so much like a fat, elderly baby herself.

At that moment a neat nurse in a cap passed the house pushing a perambulator briskly before her.

"There she is! That's the nurse!" Eliza exclaimed. "They call her a trained hospital nurse. She gets twenty-five dollars a month *and* her washing done, and if I'd had as big a family as Solomon I couldn't begin to pretend to know one half as much about babies as that woman thinks she does who's never had so much as half a one! If I had my way, oh, how quickly I'd send her flying!"

It was my first glimpse of a condition of affairs I didn't know existed.

Eliza rose to go, and sent back to me over her shoulder —

"Mark my words, that baby's head will be flat as a pancake if they don't take her up more!"

I understood everything Eliza said soon enough. In a few weeks Ellery and Jane, the baby *and* the nurse, came home for a visit. That was when I learned first-hand about "The Grandmother's Tragedy." I think all grandmothers will agree that there is a certain emotion at the sight of your first grandchild that is a little different from any other. Your son who was *your* baby only yesterday has a little son of his own.

I felt as other grandmothers do — that it was a pretty heavy responsibility for my son and that inexperienced little thing, his wife, to undertake, and I guessed that they probably were as gay and light-hearted about it as I was myself before my own children showed me what a grave thing it was to be a mother.

"Never mind," thought I, "*I'm here*, fortunately enough for them!" I was ready to pour out on them the treasures of my own experience. But more than my desire to help them, stronger than any wish I have known for years, was my longing to hold in my arms my blessed grandbaby — it was so long since I had held a baby of my very own. Yet, at the same time, it seemed almost a joke that I really was old enough, so soon, to have grandchildren. I thought in my ignorance that being a grandmother meant all the pleasure of having children and none of the care. So I planned and dreamed. Then came the reality and with it "The Grandmother's Tragedy."

I found out, as Eliza Storrs found out, and as so many women of my generation have found out, that I wasn't to have anything — neither pleasure nor responsibility. My empty, expectant arms were to remain empty. Jane's idea and the nurse's idea of a grandmother were negative; indeed, a grandmother was something to be guarded against. There was no room for a grandmother in the routine of Roger's little life. So I remained an outsider, a spectator, and a spectator who was watched to see that she didn't make herself intrusive — didn't, with her importunate affection, make an inroad on the rules laid down for the baby.

I'm afraid I took it a little hard. It was such a disappointing way of setting out on one's career of grandparent, so different from what I had looked forward to with such eagerness. There is something so heartbreaking in feeling full of love, and then having your affection set aside gently but definitely as something nobody wanted. Besides that, I worried about the baby. How many times during those three weeks I echoed Eliza Storrs, "Mark my words, that child's head will be as flat as a pancake." I longed to take him up, but actually didn't dare, though he was my own grandchild! While Jane was perfectly polite about it, she was as nervous as any old hen when I was near the baby. The reason she gave for leaving him on his back hours at a time was that it made a child nervous to be disturbed, and that a child, anyway, was not a plaything.

Elderly Woman

"Perhaps," Ellery suggested once, "he likes to be played with."

"We shouldn't consider what a child *likes*," Jane remonstrated, and I was sure she was quoting from a medical book. "We should only think what is for his good!"

So, though Roger would crow at me in the most beguiling way, Jane or the nurse was always on hand to see that we never had a word in private together.

It *was* hard work learning to be that kind of a grandmother; to my way of thinking it was being no grandmother at all. But the time came when I proved my right to love Roger in my own way. The nurse was off for an afternoon, and the baby began to cry. At first a little whimper, then a good loud roar. From the first moment it was evident to me he had an attack of colic. Jane didn't go to him at once, but continued to sew calmly. Presently she moved him over on his side and gave him a little *cold* water, but he kept on yelling, of course. Jane got up and walked the floor. Then, before my very eyes, she got down a book about babies, and read in it what to do; I wouldn't have believed it if I hadn't seen it for myself. She didn't find the right place, or else she couldn't put her mind on it, for at last she wailed out:

"Oh, what do you think is the matter? Oh, what do you think I ought to do?"

"I think you had better take him up, Jane," I said gently. I was very sorry for Jane; her outside shell of assurance and know-it-all was, after all, only a mask behind which a poor, inexperienced little mother lurked trembling. "Take him up and lay him on his stomach over a hot-water bottle. He's got a little attack of colic."

"Thank God!" said Jane. "I thought he might be going to have a convulsion!"

She was pale as a sheet, so I did it for her. I whisked him up, and comforted him just as if it had been only yesterday I had had my babies to look after. Jane watched me respectfully. She always lifted Roger warily as if she were afraid he would break. After that, discipline was relaxed. I had come into my own.

Hard as I thought my first experience was, I have learned since that it is nothing to the humiliation some grandmothers have undergone. I have heard of some who have been treated as if they were contagious diseases, and by their own daughters! I hope there are not many such; it is too sad a way of being cheated out of one's birthright. There would be fewer young mothers, I think, who mistook colic for convulsions, and looked up in books what it was their babies were crying about, if the younger generation hadn't such a contempt for our old-fashioned ways. Germs are at the bottom of that contempt, though young mothers are learning daily that there is more to being a mother than in having the bottles well sterilized.

I for one protest against the "Thou shalt nots" that are written down for grandmothers. They will, of course, pass the way of many of the other useless "Thou shalt nots." But what good will that do my generation? We shall have been defrauded of some of our rights as grandmothers, and our grandchildren will have been defrauded with us. There are some things I hold to be the right of all children from the very moment they are born, and one is the right of being spoiled by their grandparents; hand in hand with that goes the right of a grandmother to spoil them.

Age lops off our interest in one thing, then another. Year by year absence and death thin the number of our friends. Be our children never so devoted and loving, there always have been and there always will be days that have long arid places in them for people who have traveled far in the Land of Old Age. It is no one's fault. It is a part of life, no more to be complained of than the loss of the suppleness of youth. The Land of Old Age has sparsely peopled districts. Shadows move about under the shade of trees; they are the shadows of the people we used to love. Sometimes as we sit dozing in its tranquillity we hear sounds of footsteps that make our hearts beat; the sound of dear voices comes to us, and then we wake up; they are only the dear echoes from the past, the reflections of the things that were. We know that never this side of the Great Silence shall we hear them with our waking ears.

Then to us, sitting lonely and silent, come the voices of little children; living children, and not shadows that vanish if we dare to look at them full in the face. They are our children's children, and all at once the silent country wakes up to life. We know now why the Land of Old Age is so still and empty. It is so that the children may find plenty of room there to play. To me, in all the Land of Old Age there is no dearer sight than those old people you see with little children around them. Sometimes it is an old man taking his little granddaughter out to feed the hens, or again an old woman sitting happily, a little sleeping child in her arms. Do not disturb her, for she had gone back years and years, back to her own youth, and she is dreaming that she has her own baby in her arms.

In the Land of Old Age how many songs are sung every day to little children by lips that had forgotten how to sing, for, oh, so many years! There comes trooping to you a gay little procession of stories and games; they stand around you clamoring to be told and sung and played for your grandchildren. They talk about children being spoiled nowadays, what with mechanical toys and all; I am sure that it is in the homes where there are no grandmothers to cut paper dolls or teach how to make reins on a spool-and-pin knitting-machine. My little grandsons push spools around the room, playing they are automobiles, instead of *chu-chu* cars. Only last week I was called upon to make equipment for so recent a thing as the Spanish War. My boys fought the British, but I made the paper hats of just the same pattern for both generations; the swords which I forged were of two pieces of wood craftily tied together by string. My grandfather taught me how when I was a little girl.

One day soon after I had won my right to be a grandmother, I was sitting with Roger in my lap, singing him one of the baby things one croons without knowing what it is.

All at once I began to listen to myself sing, with a certain surprise, as if to some one else, and there were the foolish words I sang:

> "The craw and the poosie-o!
> The craw and the poosie-o!
> The muckle cat got up an graat
> On the top of Grannie's hoosie-o."

I hadn't thought of it for years, not since I sang it to my own babies. My mother had sung it to me, and her mother to her, because back, who knows how long ago, we had a Scottish grandmother. Now all the memory of her that there is, is this old nursery rhyme, which has survived mysteriously through the changing generations. I smiled with a certain triumph to think that the women of our family would sing "The craw and the poosie-o" to their babies when all Jane's "Thou shalt nots" had been forgotten.

Young People
and Old

The mothers of the little children do well to let them stay with their grandparents while they will, for soon enough they grow up.

There are always the ghosts of little children near older people, which teach them to understand the hearts of those other little children whom they meet in the real world. The grown-up children are so much harder to understand. They fill me with such a sense of ignorance, for they know so many things which I once knew and have forgotten. Indeed, almost the whole tissue of their lives is made up of these things.

Elderly Woman

I do not know why I remember my girl-hood so little, but I find that I am not alone in this. When I pin down my contemporaries, they have the same lapses of memory that I have myself. Perhaps it is because the serious things of life overshadow this time; marriage and children follow so closely on the heels of girlhood; one discovers so soon that so many of the things one has learned and almost all one has thought and dreamed have no place in the real world. So little, indeed, do I remember of this part of my life that I sometimes feel as if I had been married ever since I was a child in short dresses.

I find as I turn over the pages of the past — and so many of them are obliterated or contain only stray sentences of unrelated stories — that I can remember more about the way I felt when I was a very little girl than when I was a big one. Of the things that happened when I was at the young-lady age I remember so little: a dress, a party, a few faces, a confession of some fault that I was afraid to make to my mother. And when I finally came to her, after losing sleep, she took what I had to tell her — and I don't remember what it was — in a very disappointing, commonplace way.

"Well, well," said she, "I suppose every girl is bound to make a fool of herself first or last, and I oughtn't to expect you'll escape, my dear. Let's not discuss it further!"

I think my mother prolonged her life by refusing to discuss unpleasant things further.

Lately I have often run through these especial pages of my life, because it is only recently that I have realized what a gulf separates us older people from the younger ones. Perhaps all older women do not feel as I do, or perhaps they do not think about it at all, and imagine contentedly, as I did before Gertrude came on a visit, that because they love young people they know all about them.

Gertrude is my great-niece; she is spending her Easter vacation with us, and she is a sophomore in college. She is pretty, as are her charming clothes; she looks one straight in the eyes when she talks — hers are clear gray and have as much expression as those of a robin; and though it is plain to be seen that none of the things which make a woman of one have touched her, she has a calm assurance of bearing that comes from perfect health. Health, indeed, shines out of her; her vitality seems a force, and an almost overpowering one. In her presence I feel myself small and shrunken of body. She is the kind of capable modern girl who knows how to make a parent mind, and so compelling a quality is the serene assurance of youth that I felt, as I sat there beside Eliza Storrs, that, had Gertrude been my daughter, I would never have dared to face her with that last year's plumage on my hat.

My own children and I have grown up — I had almost said grown old — together, and Margaret, while she may scold me about my hat, will understand; but to Gertrude it will seem mere wanton dowdiness, a sign of age something akin to the losing of one's faculties. This is because we have no means of communication, as I found out, to my surprise, when Gertrude first arrived.

"How is your dear mother?" I asked.

Gertrude told me, and then said that they

were all so glad at home that my health was so much better than it had been the winter before. I asked her next how she liked college, and she replied she found it "broadening," and then I asked her what her studies were. I saw a little shadow of amusement cross her face; and though she answered me with polite exactness, I realized with chagrin that I had made a mistake. I felt intellectually all elbows and feet — they do not call them "studies" any more; young women of Gertrude's age speak about their "work" instead.

I find, as we grow old, we often repeat the experiences of our youth. As the world runs from me and I become less sure of my ground, I now and then have moments of extreme embarrassment in the presence of younger people — when my memory slips a cog, for instance, or when I find I have repeated the same thing twice — that is like nothing I have felt since when, as a little girl, I did things that made me long for the kindly earth to open and swallow me. The only difference is that now I can laugh off my mortification, and then I used to wash it away with tears.

Elderly Woman

After I had asked Gertrude about her studies and she had answered, we seemed to have finished definitely and for all time everything we had to say to each other. We looked at each other kindly, even with a certain affection, but, nevertheless, conversation languished and died.

"Gertrude is a lovely girl, isn't she?" Margaret said to me later. "And so responsive!" — I had heard the two chattering away like a couple of magpies.

"Gertrude and I don't speak the same language," I answered, "though we're both tolerably proficient in the English tongue when we're not together."

"Not many young girls come to the house; perhaps that's the reason," suggested Margaret.

"I'm sure," I replied, "I see a great deal of young people." For, you see, I thought it was all Gertrude's fault.

"A great deal of young people about thirty," said Margaret.

As I thought of my young friends, I found that Margaret was right; that while I had been asleep one night all my little girls that I was so proud of keeping in touch with had grown to be women "about thirty."

Since Gertrude came there have been plenty of real young people around the house. Margaret made a tea for her right away, and I had a chance to see the young people of my town, many of whom I am ready to take my oath were babies no later than day before yesterday, and I confess I still thought of them as babies. It is a long time since I have recognized all the girls who bow to me on the street, for I am absent-minded, anyway. Now I am beginning to place a few of them. The pretty girl with curls is Laura Dickinson. I remember her at ten as an active pair of dividers careering over the earth's surface; I never saw a child with such thin, lively legs. The young man who pays Gertrude especial court is John Baker. I remember very well going to see him four days after he was born. He was Sarah Baker's first grandchild, and she was inordinately proud of him. After that, the last definite recollection I have of him is the time, when, at the age of five, he broke my china jar and yelled loudly with despair over what he had done. As they were

---

named to me there was not one I did not recall as a baby, and very few that I hadn't taken for their older brothers and sisters.

How had they accomplished the process of growing up so fast, and where had they been when they were about it? That was the first thing that struck me. The next was how venerable I seemed to them. I am, as I have had occasion to mention before, what the people around here term a "mighty spry old lady," and noways infirm; but these children cannot remember a day when I was not old; they do not go back to the time when my hair was not already gray, and they give me the respect due to age. No one need tell me that among well-born young people the respect for the old is dead. These dear children fairly bristle with respect for me. If I come into the room where they are, they are full of charming little attentions in the way of easy-chairs, cushions, and footstools. Personally, I dislike soft-padded chairs. I was taught to sit upright as a girl, and I still sit so, my backbone being as strong as ever. I am never more uncomfortable than when I have several cushions tucked about me, but often of late years I have had to sit arranged in this modern way or seem ungracious. If women of Margaret's age frequently force sofa pillows on me, those of Gertrude's can hardly wait to say "good-afternoon" before they pop one behind me; old ladies and sofa cushions are in their minds inseparable.

The other day my old friend Eliza Storrs and I were coming home together in the electrics from Standish. We had been on quite a jaunt together; in fact, we had been to help each other buy our new bonnets. We had had a good time doing it, and came home with that feeling of guilty triumph that sweetened the disapproval which we knew was before us.

"I suppose," Eliza admitted to me, "that I shall never hear the last of it. *But,*" she added, with brisk decision that was a sort of dress rehearsal of the tone in which she would later say the same thing to her daughter —"*but* there's no use talking about it *now.* I've been to Standish and seen about my hat, and I'm going again!"

Her tone had a triumphant trumpeting quality to it. The truth of the matter was, Eliza had merely had three new flowers and some foliage put in her last year's bonnet; it had, furthermore, passed through the ambiguous process known as "freshening up." For my part, while I had indeed bought a new hat, the trimming on my old one being as good as new, I had used it over again. It had been more expensive in the beginning than I had intended to get; my daughter Margaret was with me when I got it, and overpersuaded me. So I, by using the last year's trimming and Eliza Storrs her last year's hat, had the feeling deep down in our hearts that we had outwitted our wise children, who are always trying to make us put more expensive things on our backs and heads than there is any need for. I think that older women often have the same guilty joy, in spending less on themselves than they should, that young women do in being extravagant.

So, borne up by the feeling that is as exhilarating for a woman of seventy as for one of twenty-seven — that of having done something she should not — Eliza and I climbed into the electric car as light of foot as our years permitted. The car was full; we had barely entered it when two young girls, after giving each other a brief glance, sprang to their feet and hustled us into their seats. This kind act was accomplished promptly and thoroughly, and I would not for one moment be so ungracious as to give the impression that I was not grateful, nor would I for a moment undervalue the small kindnesses that the young so often shower on the old. It was not their fault that the laughter died out of our eyes, and that our spirits flagged, and that even the triumph of having achieved a last year's hat seemed less amusing than it had a moment ago, while our young friends chattered as blithely, swaying to and fro as they held on to the straps, as they had before they gave us our seats.

You see, Eliza and I had taken a little vacation away from the Land of Old Age — for there is nothing so rejuvenating as playing truant, and our day's excursion had been that — and these young girls who had risen so promptly to give us their seats had led us back to our place in the world. We had forgotten for a moment that we belonged to the white-haired company who have won their right to a perpetual seat in the cars, and however welcome a seat may be, it is not so pleasant always to remember why it is our right.

I sat there watching them, and at last I asked Eliza:

"What do you suppose they are talking about?"

"Something foolish," Eliza replied, without hesitation. "The way girls go on nowadays! When I was young, children and young people were supposed to let their elders do the talking, and now it's the young folks who do *all* the talking. I declare I sometimes feel as if I never had a chance to speak."

"Oh, come now, Eliza," said I. "You can't tell *me* that you've passed your life in a state of dumbness."

For Eliza has done her share of talking in this life.

I have known Eliza since we were schoolgirls together, and I tried to remember any concrete conversation that we had, as girls, in our endless gossiping together, and I found I couldn't.

Throughout the ride the young girls didn't stop their talk for one moment, and went down the street still chatting, while I tried to piece out from the shreds my memory gave me the fabric of their conversation.

"Eliza," I said, "does it ever make you feel old when girls hop out of their seats in cars the minute they clap eyes on you?"

"Sometimes," Eliza admitted. "But," she added with decision, "it would make me feel a great deal older if I had had to stand on my two feet all the way home from Standish!"

But while I might not wish to stand so long, I would gladly do without some of the small attentions by which I am fairly snowed under the moment I come among them. And this is not the only thing that happens when I appear. Conversation stops. They go on talking, to be sure, but I know they are talking with me for an audience, and that they expurgate their talk as they go along, just as older people's talk insensibly changes when a child of twelve joins them; just as I have weeded my talk a hundred times out of respect to the young, these dear children weed their talk from respect to the old. I am aware that they have a very vivid idea of what I think the conduct and conversation of young people ought to be, and as far as they can they instinctively conform to it — when I am around. It is taken for granted not only by these very young people, but by my older young friends my daughter's age, that by virtue of my years I am a conservative, and that I am deeply pained by certain phases of modern life. It is true that I should not like to see a woman smoke, and I wish that young girls were less slangy and noisy on the street; but I realize that each generation will have phases which seem unlovely to the older generation. So, while I may have opinions of my own at variance with those of the present day, I am not as hopelessly conservative as I seem in the presence of Gertrude and her friends. I would be glad for the courage to tell them that I would rather be shocked than have this well-meant little farce played for me, but this I shall never dare, for I shall never know them well enough.

Perhaps it is the fault of us older women that the young people are so careful of our feelings. It must be that we have ourselves put so much distance between us and them. There are some of us who are too eager to tell how well-behaved we were when we were young; who have too much to say about the slovenly ways young people have of standing and sitting, and of their slangy ways of speaking, for us to meet them often on a comfortable footing. We older women have less criticism for the younger ones than older women had formerly, I think. I fancy that to-day our attitude is one easier to get on with. I don't believe I hear so much about girls being "giddy" as I used to when I was a young girl. So perhaps by the time Gertrude is an old woman the young people of her day won't be as afraid of saying something she will disapprove of as she is. Still, if she is one of those of us who don't take everything for granted, she will find the way back to her girlhood a long one.

One doesn't need to reach the Land of Old Age to smile over the things that caused one's despair when one was Gertrude's age; so it isn't to be wondered at that the dust of years obliterates all trace of the things we laughed over and cried over so long ago. And yet, while I know that the things that seem important to

Elderly Woman

Gertrude seem unimportant to me, and will be unimportant to her five years from now, by virtue of her youth and health she can make me feel my years. She can set me wondering about the girl I once was, and I sometimes have a vague shame that I remember so little.

When I look at the young girls chattering in the street, I can only wonder about what they are talking; I knew once, now I have forgotten, and there is nothing that can make me remember. If Gertrude lived here, we should get to be very good friends, and in spite of the mutual embarrassment we now cause each other, we should find a variety of things to say to each other, plenty of common ground on which to meet. Then, too, every day Gertrude would be growing older, she would be coming nearer to my point of view, and very soon we should come to understand each other, and I should wake up to find that Gertrude was thirty and married, with a couple of babies.

Chapter
X

Unspoken
Words

As soon as a young girl marries and turns into a mother, then there is that in the hearts of all of us older women which speaks to her, for among the most poignant things in our memories is the love that we bore our little children and the mistakes we made in the rearing of them.

There is a great pathos to me in the young mothers who try so earnestly to do what is best; for, however we bring up our children, we are sure to make irreparable mistakes, and as we old people look back over the long road we have traveled, we see that is has been watered by the needless tears we have shed, and worse still, those we have made our children shed because of our needless severities. Whether we were firm or whether we were lenient, we are sure to regret the course we took; for there is no mother living who at the end of her life would bring up her children over again in the same way, nor one who does not believe in her heart that she could do better a second time.

We have realized how futile our own theories of "governing children" are, and that there is very little mothers can do for their children besides trying humbly to understand them and to avoid injustices. I don't think it is possible for any mother to do more, but it is possible to do a great deal less. So those of us who have gotten to a place where certain parental firmnesses seem tyranny, and certain sorts of discipline cruelty, would be glad to have their daughters learn this before it is too late.

I remember so vividly a recent struggle Margaret had with Betty that was so like one of those I had with her. Betty and I were sitting together on the piazza. We were singing. I take solid comfort singing with Betty, for as I grow older I find it very pleasant to have some one in the world who doesn't notice how thin and wavering my notes are, and who likes to listen to my voice, worn as it is. Presently Margaret joined us.

"Mother," Betty asked, "may I go down to Annie's house —"

"No; I can't let you go to-day," interrupted Margaret; and though she spoke gently, her answer came with such promptness I knew Betty's question was a cue she had been waiting for.

"Why not?" came Betty's little whine — that sad little "Why not?" that every mother of us knows so well.

"Because you didn't come home when I told you to yesterday."

"But I *told* Annie I'd come —"

"Well, I tell you you can't," replied my daughter cheerfully.

You know what happened then, don't you? There were tears and teasing. Margaret was firm. Betty was persistent. Margaret told Betty to stop crying and Betty cried the harder. I gathered through her sobs that there was to have been lemonade. As Margaret still refused,

Elderly Woman

Betty grew defiant. I opened my mouth to say something, and then decided not to. If all the words, for only one day, which a mother of my generation *doesn't* say to her middle-aged children, were gathered together, they would make instructive reading.

At last Margaret led Betty away, saying gently, "Dear I only keep you in because I must"; and then she ended with a reproachful, "Oh, why do you make me punish you?" Which was her way of saying the old "It hurts me more than it does you."

Soon Margaret came back and sat down by me. We could hear Betty sobbing upstairs.

"The worst of it is," said Margaret, "she thinks I'm unjust."

We rocked back and forth, and for a while neither of us spoke. Little wandering airs blew the long trailing vine of the creeper to and fro. We presented to the passers-by the same spectacle of peace that Betty and I had a few moments before. But we two knew how changed things were, for the only sound in the world that we heard was that persistent, angry sobbing upstairs. I knew that Margaret's heart was wrung with it, and I suffered with her, for Margaret is my baby, and very mercifully we cannot suffer for our grandchildren's tears, or any other tears, for that matter, as we do for those of our own children.

Besides, while I was sorry for Betty, and I will tell you privately that my sympathies were with her, though I wouldn't have confessed it to Margaret — I was glad to see the little thing show so much spirit. She was protesting with all her strength against what seemed to her injustice and the abuse of power — and you can feel these things with as great indignation as any one, even though you are not old enough to call them by their names. And so, though I hate to hear a child cry, if it hadn't been for Margaret's distressed face, I should have had a certain satisfaction in hearing Betty's indignant roars.

As a baby Betty was *too* good. Margaret brought her up in the modern, cast-iron, systematic way, and her subdued whimpers of useless protest went to my heart; I used to find myself wishing she would have a good old-fashioned fit of crying, with yells that one could hear across the street. So it was a relief, as Betty grew older, to have her show a normal amount of strong will, although Margaret has been as perplexed as if the nursery clock had up and defied her. I have never dared tell Margaret how I felt about this, for there is nothing that irritates a mother of the present generation more than to have her own mother give her advice concerning the rearing of children, however much experience she may have had. Like most grandmothers to-day, I have wisely held my tongue, though sometimes it has been hard work not to speak.

Margaret was learning that while you may make rules for a baby, there is no set of rules made by man that will apply to a child of six, for Betty continued to sob defiantly. At last Margaret said:

"I have to make her mind, you know."

I nodded.

"She must learn to keep her promises."

"Of course," I assented. Poor girl, I knew she was making apologies to herself for causing Betty unhappiness.

"If I had known she cared so much —"

I nodded again. I knew so well what she felt. I also knew what I would do if I were in her place; because one is a mother is no reason why one shouldn't retire gracefully from a false position.

"But now I can't, of course —" she concluded firmly.

Again I outwardly agreed — this is one of the arts one acquires with years — but what I wanted to say was:

"Why not? Why can't you give in?"

One of the tenets of the governing of children is that when you have made a mistake, have given a too heavy punishment or imposed a command that is more distasteful than you dreamed it would be, you must persist in the matter to the end. We deal this way with our children, little and big, and unreasonable obstinacy is called "being firm." Why we feel we must act this way, I don't know. I have never known, even when I was most "firm" myself, and I don't believe any one else does. I'm sure Margaret didn't. We were silent again.

"If one could only know what one ought

to do. Oh, it's so hard to know what's right!" sighed my poor daughter at last.

In the past half-hour she had gone over the weary path every mother must travel so often. We mete out to our children what seems like justice, but justice turns its back on us and leaves us stranded with a child who is crying its eyes out because it is unjustly treated. As Margaret said, "It is so hard to know what is right."

So old women who see their little grandchildren playing about them cannot help but think of their own lost babies. Out of the past our little children look at us, and as our eyes meet theirs we falter:

"My child, I did the best I knew."

"Yes, mother." — Then, "Mother, do you remember the time you laughed at me, and because I got angry you punished me?"

You say meekly:

"I was rude that time, and then unjust, dear."

"Mother, do you remember —"

But you can't bear to listen. You know how many times you didn't do your best; the times you were gentle because you were too cow-ardly to fight; the times when you punished without understanding; the times when you im-posed too heavy penalties for childish faults — for, after all, you were no better mother than you were woman; and so you change your boast of having done your best to:

"My child, I loved you dearly always — through your mistakes and through mine."

That is the most that any mother of us can say. As we grow old, we are very apt to return in spirit to the days when our children were our very own, and wonder we didn't treasure them more. We find out, as we get along in years, that we could have been just as good mothers with fewer tears shed.

I cannot bear to think how I made Mar-garet and Helen sleep on little hard nubbins of curl-papers so they might have fluffy curls the next day — curls were the fashion then, and my children had hair as straight as a string. I hate to remember how I forced them to eat the things they didn't want to. I had a long battle with Helen over soft-boiled eggs; she would not eat them. No one was benefited by my persistence, nor could possibly have been, whichever way the battle came out; it was of no importance either way; but I made the whole household uncomfortable with the conflict. I didn't believe, in those days, in "humoring children about their food." Dear me! How many needless tears I made that child shed, and how unhappy I was over it! I thought eggs were for Helen's good, and I was bound she should eat them. I am glad to remember that in the end she won, and I can only look back and wonder at myself for my foolish persistence.

I sometimes wake up in the night and think over some of the little unkindnesses I did Margaret, or some coveted pleasure I denied my children because it was too much trouble to let them do as they wanted, and I have the same bitter regret over these things, small though they seemed at the time, that I might have had if I had lost my babies through death instead of losing them only by having them grow up into men and women. Every older woman has a sad little collection of such memories. They are among the few sad things one carries with one to the end of life, for age goes not make us forget our injustices towards our little children. We remember them always, and time, instead of softening them, makes them grow worse. Incidents that in youth seemed of little importance look very much like cruelties when we look at them from the Land of Old Age.

So I was glad when Margaret could stand it no longer and went upstairs to Betty. As she went into the room, the child burst into a fresh storm of tears. Margaret tried tenderly to calm her; but it was freedom or nothing for Betty.

So Margaret said things like: "You know you never get things by crying for them. Betty! If you speak so to me I shall have to punish you severely!"

She came downstairs again with a firm line around her mouth. I knew just how she felt. She had gone into battle, and she intended to fight it out to the end — whether it was good for Betty or not. I looked at Margaret and I felt that time had gone backward, and that Margaret was myself and Betty one of my own children, while I myself was some invisible outsider watching the same old conflict repeat itself. Most older women, as they watch their grown-up children, have this almost uncanny feeling of living over again their own mistakes and blunders. At such times one cannot help an ob scure feeling of responsibility, as if somehow it were one's own fault, so much are your daughter's mistakes your very own; at such times I cannot keep from trying to help even though I know it is unwise, so I had to say at last:

"Don't you think you are making a great deal out of a small matter?"

It was such a miserable way of wasting a bit of one's childhood and youth.

"Disobedience isn't a small matter," replied Margaret shortly.

"Carelessness is," I suggested.

"She's a very obstinate child!" Margaret asserted. By this time she had lost sight of the fact that it was the sense of injustice that made Betty obstinate.

Then, as I started to say something more: —

"Darling," Margaret interrupted with awful patience, "I've got to fight this out myself. You're only making it harder for me."

I had it on my lips to say: "It would be better for you if you allowed your mother to make a suggestion now and then!" For no one likes to be asked to hold one's tongue, however politely, and above all by one's own child. But as I looked at Margaret's careworn young face, and saw her plodding along the iron path she called duty, — in this case, as in so many others, a path which led nowhere, — my little flash of impatience died.

But my spirit cried out to her though my lips didn't speak: —

"Oh, my dear, it's no matter at all! Don't, don't feel so about it!"

Then I went away, leaving Margaret making her tragic mountain out of Betty's little molehill of carelessness; remembering in my young days how warmly I sympathized with a friend of mine whose mother always interfered in the discipline of her little grandson. Whatever he had done, "How happy he was before you disturbed him!" she would say, reproachfully.

Now I understand. There are so many sorrows and cares which we must inevitably meet as we journey toward age, and so many perplexing moments in life which we cannot

Elderly Woman

avoid, that we want, oh, so much, that our children might at least be spared and spare themselves the unnecessary worries. It is the useless mistakes and needless suffering each generation undergoes that we of the older protest against, and for which we now and then break silence, only to learn again the bitter lesson of our uselessness.

The Isolated Generation

I couldn't help Margaret that day in that one little thing any more than I have been able to help my children in the greater crises of life. I couldn't even imagine I was helping her; and this is one of the bitterest things we mothers have to bear when we get old. We have learned then that we can't help our children to lead their lives one bit better. There is not one single little stone we can clear from before their feet, be our old fingers ever so willing. With yearning hearts we see them making the mistakes we could teach them to avoid if only they would listen. We see them going through one experience after another, stumbling here, again hurting themselves against the same corner you hurt yourself against so long ago, repeating all the world-worn mistakes, while we elders watch anxiously and may not even cry out, "Take care!" Our sons repeat the follies of their fathers, our daughters make over again all the mistakes of their mothers. It is very hard to sit in silence when you see them doing all the things that you did and then so painfully learned better. We feel that we could so easily point to the fair open road if our children would let us, but we are as useless to them as guideposts to the blind. We must watch our children lose themselves in the tangle whose miseries we know so well, and see them at last, after long years of wandering, find their way back home, heart-sore and worn — and all the time we can't help thinking it all needn't have been. That, to us older mothers, is the heart-rending part of it. Instead of helping, you must sit quiet and fold your hands, knowing that if you did speak they wouldn't hear you. Your children, however dearly they love you, will think you say what you do only because you are old and have forgotten, and therefore you cannot possibly understand life as they see and live it. If you run after your children crying, "Oh, my child, don't do this," they won't listen to you, or if they do they smile at you as if you were a child. They are so sure, these young people, they know more about life than you do! Or it may very well be that instead of smiling, they have hard work not to show you how impatient they are that you have interfered in something you can't know about.

The right of free speech with our children is one of the pleasures of life which age often takes from us. When they are young they listen — they have to then — even if they go away and forget; but as they get older, they don't often let us have the illusion that we are listened to. I have even known some mothers who were not allowed to talk at all about their children's interests.

I have never understood the watchful irritation with which our grown children meet our suggestions concerning their affairs, for these are the things that lie nearest our hearts. Are they afraid, I wonder, that we will forget they are grown up? I grant it sometimes is hard to act as if one realized it.

However this may be, there are very few grown people who can bear advice from their own mothers, even though they listen patiently to all the rest of the world. I remember I had the same curious intolerance for my mother's advice, and now I am at a loss to account for my impatience. Did I fancy, I wonder, that my problems were so different from those she had solved during her long life?

There are, after all, few mothers who have grown old in the service of their children who have not some little wisdom ready to give. Some of us have learned a short road to peace; all of us have learned something that would make life easier for the children we love, but out of the fullness of our knowledge and experience we can give away not so much as a crumb. That evening I almost envied Margaret her trying afternoon; she believed, for the moment anyway, that she was doing her Betty good.

There is something very touching in the unreasonable expectation each generation has for its children. Obedience, cheerfulness, self-control, punctuality, are only a few of the virtues every young mother starts out by expecting of her babies. It only shows the serene self-confidence the young have in making the next generation better than the last. For, mind you, every mother expects to do this herself, and it's a happy time when you still have the illusion of power and still believe you can play Providence for your children, that you can bring them up very much as you choose; when you still feel that everything depends on you, and that with your love for them you will be able to defend them, not only from the world but from themselves. And so for a very little while you can. Young mothers in their tender ignorance imagine that this will always be so.

But very soon your children slip from between your fingers. They develop new traits that you don't understand and others you understand only too well, for like weeds your own faults come up and refuse to be rooted out, and you lie awake nights trying "to know what is right," still thinking that your child's welfare is in your own hand, trying with your own little strength to combat faults that are as old as your race, that are part of you and your mother and her mother before you, and will be part of your children's children. I see my daughters going valiantly to work at this hopeless task, high in courage, full of confidence that *their* children shall be saved anyway. As they bring their children up, they often talk to me about their own childhood — and very tenderly point out the mistakes I made with them. I smile one of those inward smiles age knows so well, as I gather from their accent, more than from anything they say, that they hope to avoid all my errors; and indeed that they think they have avoided a good many already.

I let them talk. The last time Henry was on a visit we talked of old times and old methods, and especially of the desultory education I gave Margaret. Henry is doing better in this respect, and my older granddaughters are on the road to becoming very learned young ladies. I only hope Henry is taking as much pains to make his girls stand up straight as I did with her. While we compared new educational methods with the faulty old ones, I couldn't help saying to my daughter: "All I hope, dear, is that when you're my age you will have as devoted a set of children."

For when your children have disproved all your theories; when none of your sons have taken up the professions you tried so hard to have them; when they have consulted their own wills in everything in life, their affection is the great recompense. If our children really love us and show us that they do, I think we may count that we have won in the game of life, and I would be glad to have my children realize this, and have it help them over the discouragement of those years after their children have apparently slipped from them altogether.

When I was a young mother I believed, too, that I could be a Providence for my children. I believed they had been given me to mould as I would, and the only limit of the influence I would have was the limit of my own strength and love. Then there came a time when I realized that every child on the street my child stopped to talk with had its share in bringing up my sons and daughters. One week in school was enough to upset all the training of years. They learned faster from their friends, and more willingly, than ever they did from me, and it seemed to me then that they learned the things they oughtn't to quickest of all. My well-brought-up little boys came from play talking loudly, making faces, playing the fool. Margaret would come home from a visit with a trunkful of affectations and an assortment of silly ideas — how silly I knew very well, for I had had those same ideas and thrown them aside myself — why I didn't get comfort out of the fact that I had outgrown these very things, and that they, too, would in time inevitably outgrow them, I don't know. It's a bad moment when one realizes that the most shallow boy and girl can have an influence over your children greater than your own, and that some thoughtless ridicule from any one your sons admire is able to undo all your patient work. It was when I saw these things that I began to see that my place in my children's lives must be very much less than I had first supposed, but I only redoubled my efforts. By that time I was past the place when commands and punishments were very much used. I used all my tact and affection and diplomacy to make children what I wanted them.

As they grew older still, I found my ideals of what I wanted them modified and changed by what they were. How much I am responsible for what they are to-day I am at a loss to decide, but I do know that the boy next door has always had a more direct and apparently a stronger influence than I ever had.

However philosophical I might be, however glibly I talked to myself about "heredity and environment," I felt deep down in my heart that I was responsible, and I alone, for what my children were. How many hours I have spent — yes, and days and months — in wondering just how I had failed. I felt that I was responsible for every one of their faults, that with more wisdom and more courage and more patience everything might have been different.

I have always envied those women who can say, "Anna gets her obstinacy from her father's family," or, "George has the Crawford temper"; but perhaps they too feel, down deep in their hearts, that they are somehow to blame for whatever is wrong. I was already an old woman before I was able to free myself of my part of the burden of responsibility, for in the end I realized that, after all, I couldn't hold myself accountable for the things that happened when they were away from me altogether. But always the torturing question remains with us mothers, "If I had done differently, could I have saved my daughter this unhappiness? If I had been firmer, couldn't I have helped my son more?"

It makes no difference what good children you have or how well they have "turned out"; mothers still ask themselves these questions, so heavily do the sins of their children weigh on them, even when they are not sins at all. I have always wondered why nothing has ever been said about the sins of the children being visited on the parents, for if our sins are visited on our children theirs are doubly hard for us to bear. After they have forgotten them we still remember, for we wonder always if we might not have prevented them by greater wisdom.

As one advances farther into the Land of Old Age, one sees more and more how isolated each generation is from the other. We begin, like Margaret, playing Providence to our children. We end, like myself, a spectator at the drama of our children's lives. You will not be able to turn the tragedy into a comedy. You can only watch it, breathless, no more able to stop the march of events than the little boy in the gallery who hisses the villain. If we mothers have helped at all, it is what we are, and not what we have taught, that has counted. Yet, though we older people know there is a gulf of time between our children and us that may not be bridged, we can't help trying to bridge it.

If you are in the thick of the play of life, look around you and you will see the gray-headed spectators who have themselves stepped off the stage. They are the mothers and fathers of the players, and each one of them is murmuring advice or encouragement to some dear child who never stops to listen. Some cry as they look on, and some laugh, and some sit proud and complacent, and in her heart each one of them knows that the words she repeats so often are not heard. But they keep on, for deeper than the knowledge of their own uselessness is the feeling of responsibility. You must bear the sins of your children until you die, just as you have your silent part in their successes. You put them in the world and you feel that you must answer to yourself for what they are.

Though each generation must work out its own salvation, we mothers can't reconcile ourselves to this knowledge. To our last days many of us go on persisting in the belief that we could help our grown-up children if they would only stop long enough to listen.

In spite of myself, I believe this. I can't help it, and I like to think that they listen more than either of us knows, and that because they love me so dearly, they hear, after all, the things I don't speak out loud. So at the end of life I can only say to myself what I wanted to say to Margaret: Each one of us can help her children, she her small ones and I my big ones, only by loving them dearly and trying humbly to understand; for I believe that only in this way can one generation come near to the other.

Lengthening
Shadows

I have spoken of us older people as spectators at the play of life, speaking words of encouragement which were not heard; and if we speak words that are not heard, so are our ears almost always on the alert to catch the inner meaning of our children's lives, to enter in and understand all the details that are kept from us.

I have a son whom I have seen but few times in many years; he lives in a distant country and can seldom come home. I have pictures of the house in which he lives. Often his face shines out to me familiarly from a strange group of people, none of whose faces I know. Often it will be a little snap-shot, and from the looks and gestures arrested in the photograph, I will see that they are friends of his. Once in a while word comes that "this is So-and-So, you know," or that "the lady beside me is Miss This or Miss That," — nothing more. I am familiar with all the outer surfaces of his life, as though I have lived out there with him. Every morning and evening when I pray for my children I go, it seems to me, almost bodily out toward him in that inner communion that we must feel when we pray intensely for those whom we love. In all the years of our separation no woman has had a more faithful child. Week after week his letters come — full letters, too; I follow him in his small journeys, in his comings and goings. I hear the old man and wife talk, that have done for him for so long, and to whose quaint pic-turesqueness he never becomes accustomed be-yond the point of appreciation. I know his tastes and his pleasures and his recreations. I know that materially he is doing well, but of his inner life, of his defeats, of his triumphs, of his travail in the stuff of his own character, I know nothing except what any one might know —

that he is a good fellow, sweet-tempered, as he always was, and that he has a certain touch of arrogance, of kind-hearted authority in his air that is not unlike Dudley's. Any one might know this who saw his picture or who heard him spoken of. But he might be going through the crisis of his life even, with his spirit in deep distress, and I am sure he would sit down, from force of habit, and write me one of his chatty and entertaining letters that make up a part of my life. If he is ill, you may be sure I hear nothing of it until he is better.

Since he cannot be with me in body it should be enough for me, I suppose, that he is in spirit with me enough so that he turns to me and gives me so much of his time. Yet it is not enough; it leaves me hungry. I never read one of his kind and charming letters without wondering: "Is all well with you, my son? Is life kind to you? Are your days lonely? Does the lack of wife and children press heavily upon you, or is the crust of selfishness settling over you so that you would not sell your small freedom of personal habits for the great gift of love which wife and children would give you? Is the blight of middle age creeping upon you, swallowing up the generosities of your youth that I knew so well? Or is your heart hungry for those children that you have never had, and is there some face dear to you beyond all others, so for want of it you must lead your life lonely as you do now?" These questions have never been answered for me, nor will they be ever. Yet sometimes it seems to me that I know as much of him as I do about those two children who have strayed familiarly through these desultory pages. They, too, are as careful to turn to me the smiling side of their lives as my son so far away from me.

It is perhaps for this that I feel nearer to my son Henry than to any of my children. He writes me seldom and then only brief communications. My knowledge of his life and comings and goings is through my daughter-in-law, but in the nature of his business he makes me brief and flying visits; he descends upon us at odd moments, which disturbs Margaret and Dudley. They try and try to make him telegraph me or write when he is coming. They think his unexpected visits disturb me; I suppose they get this from my trembling eagerness at the times when I am surprised into saying: "I think Henry is coming tonight."

And very often he comes when I think he is, and then again I am wrong, though I am superstitious enough to believe that he has thought of coming and then changed his mind when this strong feeling of his nearness sweeps over me. And when he comes I see him as he is. If he has made a good business deal or if business worries him, he says so, while Dudley and Margaret hover around like two anxious parents, trying to play Providence. If they know he is coming, they meet him first with warnings and headshakings, coaching him what to tell me and what not to tell me; and for a time he tries to be good, but before he goes, he flings out to me what is worrying or troubling him. To him I speak my mind more than to any one, and preach to him the self-control that he needs. He comes to me as he has always come, for a certain sort of strength. I give him balance and smooth him out. I am to him what I am not to any of my other children — the mother of younger years; the mother to whom to turn for advice and strength, and I leap out to meet it.

Elderly Woman

My other children — those who see me from day to day — tell me that his visits upset me, and so they do. I have been ill and depressed sometimes for two or three days when I have not been able to get him, or when his worry has been a difficult one, as I always was; as I was when they were ill; as I was through the difficult phases in the boys' developments.

Tranquillity and peace perhaps prolong life, and yet — who knows? There seems to be before us the question as to whether we shall wear out or rust out, and most of us are praying to fate that we may be allowed to wear out. Yet who can judge? I know that my children's silence, at which I often chafe, is not best for me, but perhaps it is best for them, since I cannot help them, since my anxiety only heightens theirs. When I see them cloaking their troubles with smiles; when I feel the atmosphere surcharged with anxiety, and see the cloud lift again, I often think it is perhaps self-preservation that makes them do what they call "spare me"; that to watch me troubled and broken with anxiety about their worries would be for them a double strain.

I know when Betty was ill that my trouble — though I was tranquil and though I spoke heartening words — was an added burden to Margaret. I know that for her there were two sick people in the house; that I was one, ill and suffering in spirit for the sick body of her child. And while it seems to me that silence is perhaps the hardest of all to bear, the peace it brings is good for all of us.

I have said that we should decide whether we should rust out or wear out, but perhaps that was decided for us in our youth and in our middle age, for we are continually deciding all our life long what kind of old people we are to be. Every moment of our lives we are preparing for age; carving out the faces that we are to wear; moulding and modeling and casting our characters for good or for bad; deciding if those last years — those dependent years, so full of heartbreak, so full of the giving-up of those things which make life life — shall be bearable to those closest to us.

Some years ago I began observing the various types of age about me, and it appeared to me in many unlovely guises. Often the women whom life had treated the most gently turned toward life unlovely faces — masks of discontent. I ask myself, Is life so sad that on the faces of age one should so often see such deep prints of ineradicable grief, or is it the habit of discontent, year by year, planting a wrinkle here and drawing down the mouth there?

I, who am as yet only what people call elderly, look sometimes with a certain fright at the faces which I see that are old. I see upon the street old men whose faces are carven as though in granite; the hardness of their own hard hearts is there in every line. Others I see yet more terrible — loose-mouthed and vacant-eyed, speaking of a life of indulgence of the body. They have no thoughts to carry with them to the grave; no light from the hills makes them lift up their eyes; they have forgotten the hills if ever they knew them. And the faces of the old women, how vacant are so many of them; how discontented! What furrowed brows, penned with sorrow as though their thoughts had become steeped with sadness until it had become moulded on every line of the face without. What bitterness again! And all these things bespeak a feebleness of the spirit. Day by day, as they walk on the road that leads to age, they forge out of life their own masters and the doom of those about them as well. There is something in character that seems to survive even the mind. I often call to mind the story of Emerson, who, when his mind failed and he couldn't think of words and what he wanted to say, waited with a sublime patience — sometimes waited for the word that wouldn't come. His own serenity outlived the worn-out tool that had used it for such high purposes.

I remember from the days of my early middle life an old woman who had become completely childish and rambled around the town in which she lived, a harmless and fantastic figure. Deafness was added to her other infirmities. And yet, as she went along the streets talking to herself, one caught snatches of a mind imperishably enwrapped in the kind things of life.

"What a beautiful child!" one would hear her remark. "Oh, the lovely child! . . . What a lovely day!"

This poor distraught and maimed spirit

saw beauty everywhere. She would stop a stranger on the street to know if she knew the Mrs. Grant with whom she lived. "Such a beautiful woman! So good, so good!"

Of all the lessons that come to me out of my past, the lesson of this creature, never a stalwart spirit, but, like her friend, "so good," returns to me the oftenest. She had had a heart that had been a fountain of love to all that came near her; though she had never been a woman of much brains or wisdom, yet her indestructible sweetness survived her, and this, it seems to me, is the lesson that age should bring to youth continually.

"Choose," says Age, "this face so beneficent, so sweet, so kind, or this other, written over and over with the small, mean vices of uncharitableness and littleness."

This much is to a certain degree in our hands, but what is not in our hands is the final end, the terrible and inevitable breaking-up of the powers of the body; the end that no one can tell if it shall come swiftly and mercifully or with torment for those one loves and for one's self. One can only hope here; one cannot know. And I suppose it is because of this menace that glides before us more and more closely, if we stop to think, that so many older men and women have such impatience at having clipped from them one or any of the little things that still make life the place it was. Every outer sign of age reminds us of this; every new feebleness of the body brings before us vividly the goal to which we are tending — not the goal of death, but perhaps the goal of the last years of an enfeebled and broken and useless life. I think it is this shadow that chills the hearts of those of us who have brave spirits more than the thought of death.

Growing Old Gracefully

I remember very well indeed when I began to hate to look at myself in the glass. That is the turning-point — I hated to look at myself. The women who look in the glass oftenest are not the vainest ones. Where a woman looks in the glass out of vanity once, she looks in the glass twenty times as a matter of criticism — looks to see if her hat is on straight, looks to see if her belt is doing its duty, looks to see if her skirt hangs well.

There came a time in my life when, while I was no longer young, I had a wholesome middle-aged look. I was no better looking and no worse than my neighbors, and my children encouraged vanity in me, as one's dear children very often will, by saying the sweet and familiar words: "How dear you look today, mother! I love to see mother in that dress"; or, admonishing me; "Mother, you really must have a new hat. Look at mother's hat!"

The moment comes to every woman when, instead of flushing under the approval of some masculine creature — either sweetheart or husband, according to her state of life, she sees herself mirrored in the eyes of her grownup children. You may be sure that these little children of yours, that you see now growing up around you, will in time pay you more tribute and also give you more frank criticism than any one you have ever known, devoted husband or sweetheart as he may have been.

I wear certain laces and a certain brooch because my son Dudley cares for them, certain colors because of my daughter Margaret, and I am continually in a state of border warfare with them both for trying to make me buy new things which I do not need and that are clear beyond my pocketbook. And my case is the same as that of many an elderly woman of my acquaintance; we have to fairly fight with our children not to put every penny we possess upon our backs. No young lady just coming out could hear the words from loving relatives that she needs a new dress so often as I do.

I will come back to what I was saying, there was a time in my life when because of the flattery of those I loved — and there is no flattery more far-reaching than that — I surveyed my middle-aged reflection in the glass with peace of heart. One of my daughters would inform me that she thought I was the prettiest mother in the world; the blessed part of it is, I think they really believed this was true. Then the day came when I realized that my face was old. I had been out of health, nothing very serious or alarming, but I had lost flesh and hadn't been out of doors much, and one day as I turned to meet my reflection it seemed to me that a thousand wrinkles stared out at me, that there were lines about my eyes, that my whole face was shrunken.

People speak of the terrible moment it is in a woman's life when she finds her first wrinkle. I don't believe most normal women find the first wrinkle at all. Very few of us are professional beauties; the happiness of very few of us consists in our staying in our first flush of looks forever. The average, normal, comfortable woman is too busy looking after her babies and her home about the time the first wrinkle puts in an appearance to even notice it, and, even if she does, to be disturbed, because all her contemporaries are no better off than she. The discovery of age is a different thing. I don't know if all women realize from one day to another as I do this creeping on of the hand of Time, but I think there must come a day of definite awakening. I have seen women stricken down with some illness and go to bed plump and middle-aged, and emerge, a few weeks afterwards, from the sick-room, frosted with age. I have seen sorrow rob women of the Indian summer of youth still more often. Generally it comes upon them stealthily like a thief in the night; you don't know how long it has been coming on, but little by little you find yourself "Old Mrs. So-and-So" instead of "Mrs. So-and-So."

Elderly Woman

The first wrinkle when one has children and a loving husband means nothing at all, but this look of age — it is the first cold warning of the Valley of the Shadow, it is a sign that one is actually on the road downhill, that the best days of life are over, that the activities that have made life worth living, from now on must slip more and more from one's fingers. My heart may feel as young as ever, but what good is that if my knees are rusty and going up and down stairs begins to be a burden, and I find myself tired after a little walk, and I know that never again can I go back, that not one of these wrinkles can vanish with returning health, that activities once given up have gone from us then forever.

Small wonder then that I don't like to look at my face, though it is still sweet in the eyes of my children. I don't like, I frankly confess, to be reminded of all that the wrinkles and gray hair imply. There is no vanity in this: I never was enough of a beauty to be vain about my looks, but was always glad that I could be, as my unflattering aunts used to say when I was a little girl, "well enough," and that "I would pass in a crowd." I think, indeed, I am better looking as an older woman than as a younger one. My features are of the kind that endure, my hair has taken a not unpleasing shade of gray, and yet I turn from this reflection of a not ill-looking elderly woman, not because I mind being older, but because now and then it comes quickly to me to what age and to what goal I am so fast approaching. The spacious and sunny hours, occupations to my liking, and my dear children at hand to smooth the road for me, make life a pleasant place — so I turn my face away.

Not long ago there was visiting some neighbors of ours an elderly relative. Her hair had not turned gray, but had kept a rather nondescript fluffy blond. She had also retained what is called "the figure of a girl." I expect that in reality she was a fairly angular woman under her successful millinery; anyway she lacked the comfortable roundness that comes to most women who do not grow thin with advancing years, and for my part I had rather resemble a comfortable armchair than a little spidery bentwood affair that looks as if it would blow away in a good strong wind. This woman, however,

Elderly Woman

at a little distance, gave a sad little illusion of youth. As one saw her going down the street, for instance, one would have thought her quite a young person; across the room one would have given her forty-five — forty-five dressed with a certain discreet youthfulness; and close at hand she looked very young for her age, very well preserved. This caused a good deal of comment.

"Well," said Margaret, "I'm glad you don't look like that, mother! I think it is absurd for a woman of her age with middle-aged daughters to dress the way she does."

"Yes," returned one of our neighbors, "and do you notice her complexion? It seems to me," went on this young mentor of the aged, "that women don't know how to grow old gracefully the way they used to."

I said nothing, but my heart went out to this poor lady who was struggling so valiantly to shove back the hands of the clock; and I would like to make here a little plea to you younger people. I know it is considered becoming to do what is called "grow old gracefully"; that is, to face the world with all your wrinkles, to have the courage of your gray hairs, to lay aside your favorite gay colors and put on the dark colors in which people are supposed most suitably to mourn their dead youth; I know that younger people consider that we should be willing and eager even to betray every one of the years we have lived by our actions, by our looks, by our dress, and I do not pretend that this is not the bravest part to take, but here and there we find a coward in this world, and let us not be untender. Who knows what pressure has been brought to bear? It is silly, if you like, it is lacking in intelligence to try to hide one's age, but what a tragedy it confesses, what a futile and heart-rending struggle! When I see women, as I have in the past, with foolish false fronts which didn't match their grizzling back hair, when I see youthful garments on old shoulders, I am sometimes filled with impatience and think, "Oh, you silly woman!" But I am still more filled with pity and say, "Poor woman! Sad woman! Woman on whose shoulders so heavy a burden has been laid that you cannot face the inevitable!"

I remember there lived in our town a maiden lady who kept her pretty looks so that she was like a sort of thistle-down wraith of a girl. She lived alone and on so small a stipend that no one knew how she kept soul and body together. She was one of those poor souls who had lost her lover on the eve of her marriage and forevermore mourned him.

When she died, strangers swarmed over her house. At the time of the auction there had been no one of near enough kin to take the trouble to go over the house and put away the little trivial effects of the dead which no casual eye should ever see, and so there was uncovered before the gaping town row after row of empty bottles of complexion bleach slightly tinged with pink; people laughed and gossiped and thought it was very funny. There were others who frowned, asserting that at her time of life this woman should have known better than to spend her few pennies on such folly; which was all, no doubt, very wise and true. This poor lady kept herself young only for herself. I suppose she didn't want the ghost of her dead lover to find a wrinkled old woman in place of the fresh-faced girl he had loved.

You may be sure that almost all older

women who refuse to grow old gracefully reveal some tragedy in these mistaken efforts which should cause younger people to be sorry. After all, it is growing old gracefully in the spirit that counts, and it seems to me more important as we advance in years that our spirits should be sweetened, and that we should be kinder in our outlook upon life, and that we should fight against the egotism of age, than that we should dress in a way to proclaim our years.

Perhaps my turning away from my looking-glass, and all my self-consciousness and rebellion at the advancing traces of years, are a greater sin against the true standard of growing old gracefully than those who can trick themselves into a belief that they look young and try naively to trick others.

When a young woman criticizes an older for these foibles, I do not think she is preparing herself in her heart to grow old gracefully, and yet all of us are preparing every day for what sort of old age we are going to pass. The question of growing old as one should is a very deep one. It isn't a matter of clothes; it is as deep as life itself.

Elderly Woman

When I was young I can remember certain older people whose passing through a room seemed to me like a benediction. There was one elderly relative of mine — a woman who had never married — with whom I used to pass afternoons. I don't think that I ever told her one of my troubles, great or small, but her very presence was so sweet, so gallant, so up-standing, and, withal, humorous — so like a perpetual sermon to me — that I used to come from her feeling as though I had drunk of the spring of life; and yet her life had been difficult. Report said she had turned her face from the marriage she desired to take care of an exacting mother; she had brought up a brood of younger brothers and sisters, and always she had fought against poverty, and, unflinching, faced loneliness as the years advanced. She, if you like, had grown old gracefully, and yet, had she insisted on dressing in scarlet and painting her cheeks to match her gown, she would have grown old no less gracefully, it seems to me.

I remember another time, when I was hurrying home to the bedside of a sick child, that my companion in the car was an old man, and as we traveled together many hours, he told me the story of his life. To hear him speak of his wife, who had died some years before, was a thing that made one believe in mankind; to hear him speak in a simple, refreshing way of his faith would make one, doubting, believe in God. He himself was fighting for the life of a son who had been stricken with consumption, but was winning in the fight. His brave talk and his loving attitude of mind poured I know not what strength into my own faltering spirit, and enabled me to go to the nursing that was before me with an unflinching heart, though he knew nothing of my trouble.

As I grow older, I see examples here and there of lovely and inspiring old age, and I pray that I may grow old gracefully in some image like that.

Afterword

by
Doris Grumbach

Afew years ago my partner in the book business came home from a wearying excursion to a barn in Southwest Harbor, a small town in downeast Maine. Her car was full of second-round choices from the collection she had bought, books she had rejected the first time. Among them was the book you have just read. To me, her aging friend, she said: "This looks like it might interest you."

I read *Autobiography of an Elderly Woman* with pleasure, then delight, and then with astonishment at the perspicacity, accepting good-humor, and intelligence of the anonymous writer who, in 1911, saw so clearly the problems of aging and wrote about them so honestly. No early-twentieth-century sentimentality and fustian prose clung to this story, no "the-best-is-yet-to be" nonsense. I decided that she was writing anonymously because she wished to put down some homely and sometimes painful truths about her resentment at being told by her children how to behave, where to live, and even, what to think.

Of course, not all of her complaints, or her particular situation in her old age are applicable today. In our time not too many elderly women live with a loving, well-to-do and protective — indeed, over-protective daughter — and her family, as she laments. But while the particulars of her life may differ from ours, the generalizations still pertain, especially the recognition that children who do not wish to be burdened by worry for the well-being of a parent will often prevent them from living the life they prefer to live.

What I found most poignant in the old woman's story was her recognition of the importance of control in the lives of the old, the need to make their own decisions, right or wrong, healthy or not. She writes:

Afterword

. . .What is not in our hands is the final end,
the terrible and inevitable breaking-up of the
powers of the body, the end that no one can
tell if it shall come swiftly and mercifully or
with torment for those one loves and for one's
self. And I suppose it is because of this menace . . . that so many older men and women
have such impatience at having clipped from
them one or any of the little things that still
make life the place it was.

Her worst fear is loss of independence, to end
with "an enfeebled and broken and useless life." She
sees that her greatest hope, in whatever condition, is
to keep some hold on the directive reins of her life.

The loneliness of the old, the narrator makes
clear, is not mitigated by the presence of other per-
sons:

"I live more alone and solitary among those I
love, groping in silence . . . I often think how
sweet it would have been if my husband had
lived, and we could have grown old together,
understanding and giving companionship to
each other."

She allows us to feel her sadness at becoming the child of her children, "impatient of the rules which they lay down for me, as once they were of the rules that I made for them." Gravely she asks herself, "How did this come about? When did it happen?"

Most touching is her admission that she hopes she will fall short of the picture of the ideal grandmother, "a graceful, shadowy person, sitting, her feet on a hassock, like Whistler's mother." She wants not to be thought of as "a mere ornamental nonentity . . . a sweet old lady" but rather to maintain her right to behave and dress as she wishes, indeed to commit some memorable misdeeds.

Now, what about this cultivated, authentic-sounding, feisty old lady who, it seems, sat down to write anonymously about her life? Who was she? Not an old lady at all, it turns out, but a well-known (in her time) professional journalist named Mary Heaton Vorse. She was born in New York City in 1874 and published *Autobiography of an Elderly Woman* when she was thirty-seven. A free-spirited, bohemian woman by instinct, she lived in Greenwich Village and Provincetown, Massachusetts with the first of her three husbands, Albert Vorse, and with him founded a club that experimented in cooperative living. Her strong views about the wrongs of society toward the poor and the working class, and women's right to vote, were formed early; she was to make her living as a radical, socialist, professional writer for such publications as *The Nation, New Republic,* and *The Masses,* of which she became editor.

Autobiography . . . was her fourth book and her second novel. For a novel it was, not a book of auto-biographical non-fiction. It was written in her mother's voice, not her own. The fictional narrator is a character in a small but meaningful cast comprising a middle-class family making its beneficent demands upon their beloved old relative. She inhabits a corner of a society in the first years of the twentieth century in which the old walk decorously (or are driven) along narrow paths and are obedient to the wishes of others. She represents that portion of the population (much smaller than it is now) whose rights are not recognized, whose physical selves are decaying, whose illnesses are irreversible, but who accept their fate with a good deal of self-deprecating grace.

I have no way of knowing how many copies of this book the publisher Houghton Mifflin was able to sell in 1911. Not too many, I suspect, since there is no record of a second printing. But I find myself

Afterword

hoping that this new edition will do better, will teach the grown children of the elderly something about the plight of their dependents, and the elderly that they are not alone, indeed, have not been alone since Mary Heaton Vorse wrote this moving and persuasive book about them.

Sargentville, Maine